November 1985

The Inheritors

The Inheritors

FRENCH STUDENTS AND THEIR RELATION TO CULTURE

Pierre Bourdieu and
Jean-Claude Passeron

TRANSLATED BY RICHARD NICE

The University of Chicago Press
CHICAGO AND LONDON

THE UNIVERSITY OF CHICAGO PRESS, CHICAGO 60637
THE UNIVERSITY OF CHICAGO PRESS, LTD., LONDON
© 1979 by The University of Chicago
All rights reserved. Published 1979
Printed in the United States of America
83 82 81 80 79   5 4 3 2 1
Published originally as *Les héritiers: Les étudiants et la
culture*. © 1964 by Les Editions de Minuit

PIERRE BOURDIEU is director of the Centre de Sociologie
Européenne at the Ecole des Hautes Etudes en Sciences
Sociales. JEAN-CLAUDE PASSERON is professor at the
Université de Paris VIII. Together, they have written *Les
étudiants et leurs études, La reproduction, Rapport
pédagogique et communication* (with M. de Saint-Martin),
and *Le métier de sociologue* (with J. C. Chamboredon).

Library of Congress Cataloging in Publication Data

Bourdieu, Pierre.
     The inheritors.

     Translation of Les héritiers, les étudiants et la
culture.
     1. College attendance—France. 2. Students' socio-
economic status—France. I. Passeron, Jean-Claude,
joint author. II. Title.
LC148.B613   378.1′98′0944   78-31532
ISBN 0-226-06739-4

Contents

Preface to the American Edition

ONE MIGHT APPLY TO *THE INHERITORS* A phrase often heard during the events of May 1968: "This is only the beginning." Fifteen years after the book first appeared, its chief virtue seems to me to lie in the effort it makes to hold together aspects of the social world which the traditions and divisions of social science tended to keep apart, such as analysis of drop-out and analysis of the functions and functioning of the educational system, or analysis of the differential reception of academic language and culture and analysis of class cultures. In particular, *The Inheritors* was intended to mark a break with the prevailing tradition in the sociology of education and to outline a program for a sociology of cultural reproduction as a dimension of social reproduction. To show what followed, one would need to refer to all the empirical work that has been done in fifteen years on all aspects of the French educational system and its relationship with cultural production and consumption and with economic production and the social structure. But rather than compile that sort of "trend report," it seemed preferable to conclude this volume with a shortened version of a recent article representing one of the directions in which research on the educational system has led.

PIERRE BOURDIEU
Paris 1979

Prefatory Note

THIS ESSAY IS MAINLY BASED ON A PROGRAM OF surveys carried out in the context of the work of the Centre de Sociologie européenne (Center for European Sociology), the full results of which have been published elsewhere,[1] on statistics from the INSEE and the BUS,[2] and on monographic studies or preliminary surveys carried out by us or, under our direction, by sociology students in Lille and Paris, working individually or in university research groups. These were on: students' mutual acquaintance (Lille group); examination anxiety (B. Vernier); an attempt at integration (Lille group); students' leisure (G. Le Bourgeois); students' image of the student (Paris group); and the Sorbonne Greek Drama Society and its audience (Paris group).

In our analyses we are particularly concerned with Arts students; we have only rarely drawn on various other surveys dealing with the whole student population or other faculties (students and politics, the users of Lille University Library, medical students, female students). The reason for this is that, as will be seen, Arts students exhibit in an exemplary way the relation to culture which we took as our object of study.[3] We realize that by isolating an analysis of cultural privilege, from within a whole set of current research projects on education and culture, we may appear to be reducing the whole range of possible questions to one single question. But this was a risk that had to be taken, in order to grasp the fundamental problem which the ritual problematic in this area almost always manages to conceal.

Paris, September 1964.

Translator's Note
DURING THE PERIOD OF THIS STUDY (before the restructuring which ensued from the events of May 1968), French

ix

universities consisted of a number of faculties—the faculties of Law, Medicine, Pharmacy, and Science, and the *Facultés des Lettres*. The latter, containing institutes for the study of literature, modern and classical languages, philosophy, sociology, and so on, corresponded approximately to departments of humanities and social sciences. For the sake of brevity, they are referred to here by the British term "Arts faculties." Admission to the faculties was, in principle, open to all holders of the *baccalauréat*, but the subsequent drop-out and failure rates were generally high.

By contrast, the parallel system of advanced professional schools —the *grandes écoles* and engineering schools—operate a *numerus clausus* which, together with the career prospects that they tend to guarantee, gives rise to intense competition to enter. Most prestigious academically are those leading to the teaching profession (the *Ecoles Normales Supérieures*) and government service (the *Ecole Polytechnique*).

1·Selecting the Elect

AMONG NORTH AMERICAN INDIANS, VISION behavior was highly stylized. The youth who had not yet "sought a vision" usually was exposed to many accounts of other men's visions, accounts that described in detail the kind of experience that would be regarded as a "true vision" and the kind of special occurrence . . . that validated a supernatural encounter, and thereafter gave the visionary power to hunt, to lead a war party, and so on. Among the Omaha, however, folk tales gave no details of what visionaries had seen. On closer examination it became clear that the vision had not been a mystical experience democratically open to any seeker but rather was a carefully guarded method of ensuring the inheritance within certain families of membership in a medicine society. Entrance to the society nominally was validated by a freely sought vision, but the dogma that a vision was an unspecified mystical experience that any young man could seek and find was balanced by a carefully guarded secret of what constituted a true vision. Young men who were eager to enter the powerful Mide society would go into the wilderness, fast, return and tell their visions to the old men, only to be informed—if they were not members of the elite families—that their vision was not authentic.

Margaret Mead, *Continuities in Cultural Evolution*

Others have observed and deplored the fact that the various social classes are very unequally represented in higher education. But is the question of educational inequality thereby disposed of? When it is pointed out, again and again, that industrial workers' children make up only six percent of the student population, is the statement made merely to demonstrate that the student world is a bourgeois one? Or could it be that by substituting a protest against the situation for the situation itself, people are endeavoring, suc-

1

cessfully in most cases, to persuade themselves that a group that can protest against its own privilege is not a privileged group?

Undoubtedly, at the level of higher education, the initial educational inequality between the various social strata first appears in the fact that they are very unequally represented there. But it immediately has to be added that the proportion of students from the various classes only very partially reflects the full extent of educational inequality, since the social categories most strongly represented in higher education are also those least represented in the active population. An approximate calculation of the chances of university entrance according to father's occupation shows that they range from less than one percent for children of farm workers, to almost seventy percent for children of industrialists, and more than eighty percent for children of professionals. These figures show clearly that the educational system objectively effects an elimination which is steadily more thorough, the less privileged the social class. But other, more hidden forms of educational inequality are less often noticed, such as the relegation of working-class or lower-middle-class students to certain disciplines, or the fact that they fall behind and mark time in their progress through school.

The chances of entering higher education can be seen as the product of a selection process which, throughout the school system, is applied with very unequal severity, depending on the student's social origin. In fact, for the most disadvantaged classes, it is purely and simply a matter of *elimination*.[1] A senior executive's son is eighty times more likely to enter a university than a farm worker's son, and forty times more likely than an industrial worker's son; and he is twice as likely to enter a university as even a lower-rank executive's son. These statistics make it possible to identify four levels of utilization of higher education: the most deprived categories have at present scarcely more than a token chance of sending their children to university (less than five percent); some intermediate categories (clerical workers, artisans, shopkeepers), whose share has increased over the last few years, have a ten to fifteen percent chance; for lower-rank executives, the chances are doubled (to almost thirty percent), and they are doubled again for senior executives and members of the professions, who have an almost sixty percent chance. Even if they are not consciously assessed by those concerned, such substantial variations in objective educational opportunity are expressed in countless ways in everyday perceptions and, depending on the social milieu, give rise to an image of higher education as an "impossible," "possible," or "natural" future, which, in turn, plays a part in determining educational vocations. The experience of their academic future cannot be the same for a senior executive's son, who, with a *better than one in two* chance of going to university, necessarily encounters higher education all around him, even in

TABLE 1. **Educational Opportunity and Social Origin** (1961–62)

Parents' Occupational Category		Objective Chances (probability of access)	Conditional Probabilities				
			Law	Science	Arts	Medicine	Pharmacy
Farm workers	M	0.8	15.5	44.0	36.9	3.6	0
	F	0.6	7.8	26.6	65.6	0	0
	Both	0.7	12.5	34.7	50.0	2.8	0
Farmers*	M	4.0	18.8	44.6	27.2	7.4	2.0
	F	3.1	12.9	27.5	51.8	2.9	4.9
	Both	3.6	16.2	37.0	38.1	5.6	3.1
Domestic servants	M	2.7	18.6	48.0	25.3	7.4	0.7
	F	1.9	10.5	31.1	52.6	4.7	1.1
	Both	2.4	15.3	41.3	37.0	5.5	0.9
Industrial workers	M	1.6	14.4	52.5	27.5	5.0	0.6
	F	1.2	10.4	29.3	56.0	2.6	1.7
	Both	1.4	12.3	42.8	39.9	3.6	1.4
Clerical workers	M	10.9	24.6	46.0	17.6	10.1	1.7
	F	8.1	16.0	30.4	44.0	6.1	3.5
	Both	9.5	21.1	39.4	28.6	8.6	2.3
Industrial and commercial proprietors*	M	17.3	20.5	40.3	24.9	11.0	3.3
	F	15.4	11.7	21.8	55.7	4.8	6.0
	Both	16.4	16.4	31.8	39.1	8.1	4.6
Lower-rank executives	M	29.1	21.0	38.3	30.2	8.5	2.0
	F	29.9	9.1	22.2	61.9	3.4	3.4
	Both	29.6	15.2	30.5	45.6	6.0	2.7
Professions and senior executives	M	58.8	21.8	40.0	19.3	14.7	4.2
	F	57.9	11.6	25.7	48.6	6.5	7.6
	Both	58.5	16.9	33.3	33.2	10.8	5.8

*In both cases these are purely *statistical categories*, including very different social groups. The category "farmers" (*agriculteurs*) includes all those who run farms, whatever the size of the holding, and the category "industrial and commercial proprietors" (*patrons de l'industrie et du commerce*) includes—in addition to independent craftsmen and shopkeepers—industrialists, who could not be set apart in these calculations but who can be shown to be among the most intensive users of higher education (see appendix I, table 1.9). A prudent reading of the table would therefore attach more significance to the most homogeneous categories.

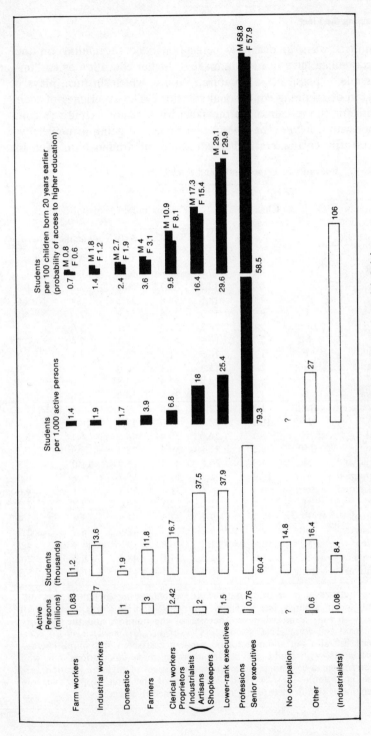

Fig. 1. Educational Opportunity and Social Origin

his family, and perceives it as a commonplace destiny; and, on the other hand, for an industrial worker's son who, with a *less than two-in-a-hundred* chance of university entrance, forms his image of students and university education on the basis of impressions filtered through intermediate persons or situations.

When it is borne in mind that extra-familial relationships are more extensive at higher levels of the social hierarchy, while remaining socially homogeneous in each case, it is clear that the subjective expectation of entering university tends, for the most disadvantaged, to be even lower than the objective chances.

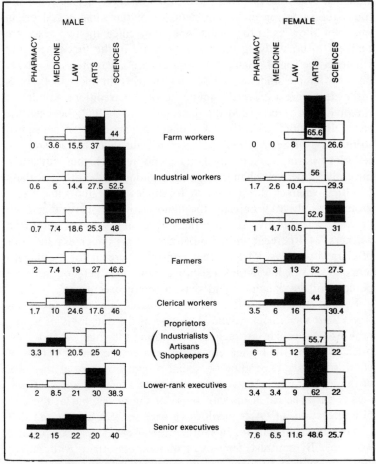

Fig. 2. Probability of Entering a Given Discipline, by Social Origin and Sex

Within this unequal distribution of educational opportunity by social origin, male and female students are, roughly speaking, on equal terms. But the slight disadvantage of the women is more clearly marked in the lower classes. While, overall, women have a slightly better than 8 percent chance of university entrance, as against 10 percent for the men, the gap is greater at the bottom of the social hierarchy, whereas it tends to diminish or disappear for the sons and daughters of senior and lower-rank executives.

Educational disadvantage is also expressed in the *restricted choice* of disciplines reasonably available to a given category of students. Thus, the fact that the chances of university entrance are much the same for males and females of the same social origin must not allow us to forget that once they enter, the two sexes are unlikely to be studying the same subjects. In the first place, and whatever the social origin, Arts subjects are always the most likely ones for female students and Science subjects the most likely ones for males: here we see the influence of the traditional model of the division of labor (and the distribution of "gifts") between the sexes. In a more general way, females are more often consigned to the Arts or Science faculties, which train them for a career in teaching. Farm workers' daughters who reach higher education have a 92.2 percent chance of going into one or the other of these faculties, whereas the likelihood for males from the same background is only 80.9 percent; the figures are 85.3 percent and 80 percent, respectively, for the daughters and sons of industrial workers, 74.4 percent and 63.6 percent for the daughters and sons of clerical workers, 84.1 percent and 68.5 percent for the daughters and sons of lower-rank executives, and 74.3 percent and 59.3 percent for the daughters and sons of senior executives.

Female students' choices are more limited, the more disadvantaged their social background. The case of the daughters of lower-rank executives can be seen as illustrating the logic whereby the price of access to higher education is a restriction of choice of varying severity depending on social origin. For it is at the level of the lower-rank executives that female students' chances of university entrance catch up with those of the males, but at the cost of a relegation into Arts faculties (a 61.9 percent likelihood) that is more marked than for any other social category (except farm workers). By contrast, females of upper-class origin, with similar entrance chances to men, are less automatically forced into Arts faculties (a 48.6 percent likelihood).

As a general rule, restricted choice applies more to the lower classes than to the privileged classes and more to female than male students, the disadvantage being more marked for females when their social origin is lower.[2]

Whereas the disadvantage of being female is mainly expressed in relegation to the Arts faculties, the disadvantage of low social origin is ultimately more fraught with consequences, since it is manifested both in the complete elimination of children from the underprivileged strata and also in the restricted choices available to those who manage to escape elimination. Thus, these students must accept the obligatory choice between Arts and Science as the price of their entry into a university which, for them, has two doors instead of five: sons and daughters of senior executives have a 33.5 percent probability of going into Law, Medicine, or Pharmacy, compared with 23.9 percent for the sons and daughters of lower rank executives, 17.3 percent for the sons and daughters of industrial workers, and 15.3 percent for the sons and daughters of farm workers.

But the conditional chances of students from a given social category enrolling in an Arts faculty give only a blurred picture of the *relegation* of pupils from the least privileged classes. Here a second phenomenon interferes with the first: the Arts faculty, and, within it, disciplines like sociology, psychology, or modern languages, can also serve as a *refuge* for students from the most intensively enrolled classes, who, being socially "required" to go to college, gravitate, in the absence of any positive vocation, toward studies such as these, which provide them with at least an appearance of academic respectability. The proportion of Arts students from a given social category, therefore, has an ambiguous significance because the Arts faculty may be a forced choice for some and a refuge for others.

If it is true that the unequal accessibility of the various disciplines leads to the phenomenon of relegation, then the hierarchy of higher education institutions may be expected to lead to the monopolizing of the top establishments by the most privileged students. And, indeed, it is at the Ecole Normale Supérieure and the Ecole Polytechnique that one finds the highest proportion of students from privileged class backgrounds, with, respectively, 57 percent and 51 percent of their students being the sons of senior executives and members of the professions, and 26 percent and 15 percent sons of lower-rank executives.[3]

The final manifestation of educational inequality, the failure of students from the most deprived classes to advance in their studies, through having to repeat grades, is found at all levels of schooling. Thus, the proportion of students of the modal age (that is, the age most common at that level) declines as one moves toward the most underprivileged classes, with the proportion of lower-class students tending to rise in the oldest age groups.[4]

If it is true that the obligatory choice of Arts or Science faculties is a manifestation of the educational disadvantage suffered by students from the working and lower middle classes (even when they succeed in experiencing this destiny as a vocation), if it is also true that enrollment in Science faculties seems to be less related to social origin,[5] and if it is granted that the influence of social origin is most clearly manifested in the teaching of the "Humanities," then it seems legitimate to see Arts faculties as the arena par excellence in which to study the operation of the cultural factors at work in the process of educational inequality, of which statistics, with their synchronic cross-sections, show only the final outcome, in the form of elimination, relegation, or late arrival. For, paradoxically, those most disadvantaged culturally suffer their disadvantage most severely precisely in the situations to which they are relegated as a result of their disadvantages.

Economic obstacles are not sufficient to explain how "educational death rates" can differ so widely between one social class and another. Even if there were no other evidence and if we knew nothing of the numerous and often very indirect ways in which the school system steadily eliminates children originating from the least privileged backgrounds, proof of the magnitude of the cultural obstacles which these children have to overcome could be found in the fact that even at the level of higher education, one still finds differences in attitude and ability that are significantly related to social origin, although the students whom they differentiate have all undergone fifteen or twenty years of the standardizing influence of schooling, and although the most underprivileged of them have only escaped elimination thanks to their greater adaptability or to a more favorable family environment.[6]

Of all the differentiating factors, social origin is doubtless the one whose influence bears most strongly on the student world, more strongly, at any rate, than sex or age, and certainly more than any clearly perceived factor, such as religious affiliation.

Though religion is the basis for one of the most obvious cleavages and though the opposition between practicing Catholics and the rest has an important classificatory function,[7] religious affiliation and even regular observance do not give rise to significant differences, at least in regard to education and academic culture. It is true that membership in religious groups or movements (especially Catholic ones) provides students, especially women, with an opportunity for organized, regular contacts within relatively integrated secondary groups—"circles," "clubs," and "societies"— which are an extension of their family environment. It is true that more Catholic students went to private secondary schools (51 percent, compared to 7 percent for non-Catholics). It is true that ideological or philosophical commitments are significantly linked to religious denomination and level of observance— 43 percent of those Catholics who identify with a school of thought name personalism and only 9 percent Marxism, with 48 percent declaring themselves existentialists; whereas 53 percent of the non-Catholics name Marxism, only 7 percent personalism, and 40 percent existentialism. It is true that Catholic students seem to invest their studies and their conception of their future careers with an ethic of goodwill and of service to others, to which female students give a particularly lyrical expression. But, in specifically academic behaviors and attitudes, religious affiliation never gives rise to statistically significant differences.

In a microcosm which is annually renewed and in a system which sets a preeminent value on precocity—age, and, more precisely, seniority, do not have their usual significance. No doubt there are behaviors, attitudes, and opinions in which the generic influence of aging can be detected: this would explain why political and student-union commitment increases with age, or why older students are more likely to live in private lodgings and to have jobs while studying. But a number of phenomena seem, on the contrary, to be linked to what might be called *scholastic age*, that is, the relation between real age and the modal age of students at the same level of schooling. While it is easy to isolate the behaviors and attitudes that are subject to the influence of ordinary aging, which increases maturity and the inclination toward independence, it is much harder to grasp the significance and influence of *scholastic aging*, because old students are not just students who have grown older, but a category of students which is represented in all age groups (and to varying degrees in all social

TABLE 2. Statistics of Social Origin of Students in Grandes Écoles (1961–62)

PARENTS' OCCUPATION (occupation of head of household or of mother or guardian)*	Polytech-nique	Centrale	Des mines (3)	Sup. Aero.	Sup. élec.	Chimie E.N.S.I. (14)	Nat. Arts et Mét.	I.N.S.A. Lyon.
0. FARMERS	1	2	5	5	4	5	5	6
Landowning farmers	1	2	3	4	3	3	5	2
Tenant farmers, sharecroppers bailiffs			2	1	1	2		4
1. FARM LABORERS							1	1
2. INDUSTRIAL AND COMMERCIAL PROPRIETORS	13	12	13	31	19	19	19	18
Industrialists	5	3	4	18	6	5	4	2
Artisans	2	2	3	4	3	4	9	7
Shopkeepers	6	7	6	9	10	10	6	9
3. PROFESSIONS AND SENIOR MANAGERIAL	57	47	41	33	42	30	19	19
Liberal professions	16	7	9	13	11	7	3	4
Professors (private sector) Professors (public sector)	8	4	10	4	3	3	2	3
Senior executives (private sector)	14	20	11	5	11	10	8	5
Senior executives (public sector)	19	16	11	11	17	10	6	7
4. LOWER MANAGERIAL	15	18	18	19	17	19	19	16
Primary teachers (private sector)	2							
Primary teachers (public sector)	7	5	4	4	4	5	5	6
Lower-rank executives (public sector)	3		8	11	5	7	6	4
Lower-rank executives (private sector)	3	13	6	4	8	7	8	6
5. CLERICAL	8	9	12	8	8	11	10	16
Office clerks	5	9	11	7	6	7	7	13
Store clerks	3		1	1	2	4	3	3
6. INDUSTRIAL WORKERS	2	2	5	2	7	7	17	14
Foremen		1	1	1	2	2	5	2
Semi-skilled	2		4	1			11	11
Unskilled		1			5	5	1	1
7. DOMESTIC SERVANTS					1	1	2	2
8. OTHER	3	4	1	1		3	3	5
9. PRIVATE INCOME, NO OCCUPATION	1	6	5	1	2	5	5	3
TOTALS	100	100	100	100	100	100	100	100

* In the case of retired or deceased parents, we have indicated the last occupation practised.

Source: *La Documentation française* n. 45, 1964.

E. N. S.		ECOLES			AGRICULTURE			% of working population 1954	Social origin of 100 faculty students†
Ulm & Sèvres	Fontenay, St.-Cloud	Inst. Et. Pol. (5)	H.E.C.	Ec. sup. com. (12)	Inst. nat. agro.	Ec. nat. agro. (3)	Ec. nat. vétér. (3)		
1	7	8		4	20	28	15	20.8	6
	5	7		3		26			
1					20		15		4
1									
	2	1		1		2			2
	1							6	
9	14	19		32	37	15	19	12	18
2		8		12		3	2		5
2	7	3		3	18	2	2		4
5	7	8		17	19	10	15		9
51	18	44		34	29	22	30	2.9	29
7		15		8	9	4	14		10
7		1							1
26	9	2		1	8	3			
4	3	15		17			4		5
					12	8	3		7
7	6	11		8		7	9		6
26	24	13		14		18	10	5.9	18
1						4			1
		3							
13	14			2			5		5
5	6	7		6		6	4		5
7	4	3		6		8	1		7
5	10	8		5	7	4	11	10.9	8
3	7	5		3		3	9		5
2	3	3		2	7	1	2		3
3	15	2		5		5	2	33.8	6
1	3	1		2		1			2
2	12	1		3		4	2		3
									1
	2	1				1		3.6	1
1	4	2		1		2	8		8
4	5	3		5	7	5	5	4.5	6
100	100	100		100	100	100	100	100	100

† For comparison.

For abbreviations see p. 12.

classes) and which is predisposed by certain educational characteristics to "age," relative to other students, in its passage through the school system.[8] Finally, the influence of age never works in a univocal way in the different areas of life, especially with respect to individuals from different social backgrounds engaged in different studies; seniority may, as we have seen, be an aspect of social handicap or, on the contrary, the privilege of the "eternal student."

Social origin—which defines totally different opportunities, living and working conditions—is, of the determinants, the only one whose influence extends to all areas and all levels of students' experience, and first and foremost to their conditions of existence. Dwelling place and the type of daily life associated with it, financial resources and their allocation to various types of expenditure, the intensity and modality of the sense of dependence, variable according to the source of finance, as are the nature of the experience and values associated with obtaining this finance, depend directly and strongly on social origin, while at the same time transmitting its influence.

How can one speak, even by way of a simplification, of a common "student situation" to designate a world in which their families ensure the subsistence of only 14 percent of those students who are the children of peasants, industrial workers, office workers and lower management and of more than 57 percent of the children of senior executives or professionals, while 36 percent of the former, and only 11 percent of the latter, are forced to take jobs while studying? The nature or amount of their resources and, consequently, their degree of dependence on their families, radically separate students according to their social origins. Not only do

---

ENS	Ecoles Normales Supérieures
Sup. Aéro.	Ecole Nationale Supérieure de l'Aéronautique
Sup. Eléc.	Ecole Nationale Supérieure d'Electricité
Chimie	Ecoles Nationales Supérieures de Chimie
E.N.S.I.	Ecoles Nationales Supérieures d'Ingénieurs
Nat. Arts et Mét.	Ecole Nationale des Arts et Métiers
I.N.S.A. Lyon	Institut National des Sciences Appliquées (Lyon)
Inst. Et. Pol.	Instituts d'Etudes Politiques
H.E.C.	Ecole des Hautes Etudes Commerciales
Ec. sup. com.	Ecoles Supérieures de Commerce
Inst. Nat. Agro.	Institut Nationale Agronomique
Ec. Nat. Agro.	Ecoles Nationales d'Agronomie
Ec. Nat. Vétér.	Ecoles Nationales Vétérinaires

they range from 200 to 900 francs a month, but incomes have
widely varying significance, depending on the scale of the supple-
mentary subsidies provided (for example, a student's clothes may
or may not be supplied by his family) and on the source of the
money. Finally, students who live at home are only partly students. They may well take every opportunity to share the student
situation, but in this choice, which they can always revoke, they
are identifying more with a fascinating image than with a real
situation and its real constraints. Depending on their area of study,
between 10 and 20 percent of the sons and daughters of peasants
and manual workers live at home, whereas the figure is 50 and
sometimes 60 percent for students (especially girls) from the
upper classes.[9]

These differences are too obvious to be called into doubt. And
so it is to students' university activity that people generally look
for the basis of the definition that might safeguard the idea that
the student situation is a single, unified, or unifying one. However
different they may be in other respects, students considered from
the point of view of their specific role do indeed share the common feature that they study, that is, that, even in the absence of
attendance or exercises, they undergo and experience the subordi-
nation of their occupational future to an institution which, by
means of the diploma, monopolizes an essential means of social
success. But students may have practices in common without it
necessarily following that they experience them identically, still less
collectively.

Students are not only users but also products of the educational
system, and no social category is more strongly marked in its
present behaviors and abilities by its past acquisitions. As much
research has shown, social origin exerts its influence throughout
the whole duration of schooling, particularly at the great turning
points of a school career. The awareness that higher education
(especially in certain disciplines) is expensive and that some occupations can only be undertaken by those with wealthy parents,
unequal knowledge about courses and the careers they lead to, the
cultural models which associate certain occupations and certain
educational options (Latin, for example) with a particular social
background, and the socially conditioned predisposition to adapt
oneself to the models, rules, and values which govern the school
system, in short, the whole set of factors which make pupils feel
and seem to be "at home" or "out of place" in school, result—
other abilities being equal—in an unequal rate of scholastic

achievement between the social classes, especially in those disciplines which presuppose previously acquired intellectual tools, cultural habits, or income. It is known, for example, that educational
achievement is strongly dependent on the (real or apparent) ability to manipulate the abstract language of ideas and that the students most successful in this area are those who have studied
Greek and Latin.[10] Thus, the present success or failure which students and teachers (with their propensity to think in terms of the
academic year) tend to impute to the immediate past, if not to
talent or essential personality, can be seen to depend on early
"options" which are, by definition, the work of family background.
Thus, the direct influence of the cultural habits and the dispositions inherited from the original milieu is amplified by the multi-
plier effect of the first scholastic streamings and channelings (themselves produced by the primary determinisms), which trigger the
action of secondary determinisms, which are all the more potent
because they expressed in the specific logic of schooling, in the
form of sanctions which consecrate social inequalities while apparently ignoring them.

In a student population, we are dealing with the final outcome
of a whole set of influences that stem from social origin and have
been exerted over a long period. For students from the lower
classes who have survived elimination, the initial disadvantages
have evolved: their social past has been transformed into an educational handicap through relay mechanisms such as early, often
ill-informed decisions, forced choices, or lost time. For example,
in a group of Arts faculty students, the proportion of students
who have studied Latin at secondary school varies from 41 percent for the sons of farm workers and farmers to 83 percent for
the sons of senior executives and members of the professions,
which is sufficient to demonstrate *a fortiori* (in the case of Arts
students) the relationship between social origin and the classical
languages, with all the attendant scholastic advantages. A further
index of the influence of family background is seen in the fact
that the proportion of students who say they followed their family's advice about the choice of subjects for the first or second part
of the *baccalauréat* rises with social origin, whereas the teacher's
role correspondingly declines.

Similar differences are found in attitudes toward education.[11]
Either because they hold more strongly to the ideology of "gifts"
or because they believe more strongly in their own giftedness (the

two tend to go together), students of bourgeois origin, while recognizing as unanimously as others the existence of techniques for intellectual work, evince greater disdain for those which are commonly regarded as incompatible with the romantic image of intellectual adventure, such as use of a card index or a timetable. Even the subtle modalities of their vocation or the conduct of their studies reveal the more gratuitous character of upper-class students' intellectual commitments. Whereas bourgeois students, more assured of their vocations or their abilities, express their real or alleged eclecticism and more or less fruitful dilettantism in the greater diversity of their cultural interests, other students manifest greater dependence on the university. When sociology students are asked whether they would rather study their own society or Third World countries and anthropology, the choice of "exotic" themes and fields becomes more frequent as social origin rises. Similarly, if the most privileged students are most attracted by fashionable ideas (seeing, for example, the study of "mythologies" as the object par excellence of sociology), this is perhaps because their previously protected experience predisposes them to aspirations guided more by the pleasure principle than by the reality principle and because intellectual exoticism and formalistic purity are the symbolic, that is, ostentatious and innocuous, way of liquidating a bourgeois experience while expressing it. The formation of intellectual mechanisms such as these surely presupposes exposure—over a very long period—to the economic and social conditions of free and gratuitous choices.

If dilettantism in the pursuit of their studies is more especially a feature of students of bourgeois origin, this is because, being more assured of preserving a place for themselves, albeit a fictitious one, at least in a "refuge" discipline, they are able, without any real risk, to manifest a detachment which precisely presupposes a greater security. They read fewer books directly linked to the syllabus, and the books they read are less "academic"; they are the students most likely to follow several different courses simultaneously, in remotely related subjects or different faculties; they are always the ones most inclined to judge themselves indulgently and, as the statistics of examination results show, this greater self-assurance wins them a considerable advantage in many situations—orals, for example.[12] It would be a mistake to see bourgeois students' lesser dependence on scholastic disciplines as a disadvantage offset by other privileges. On the contrary, a shrewd

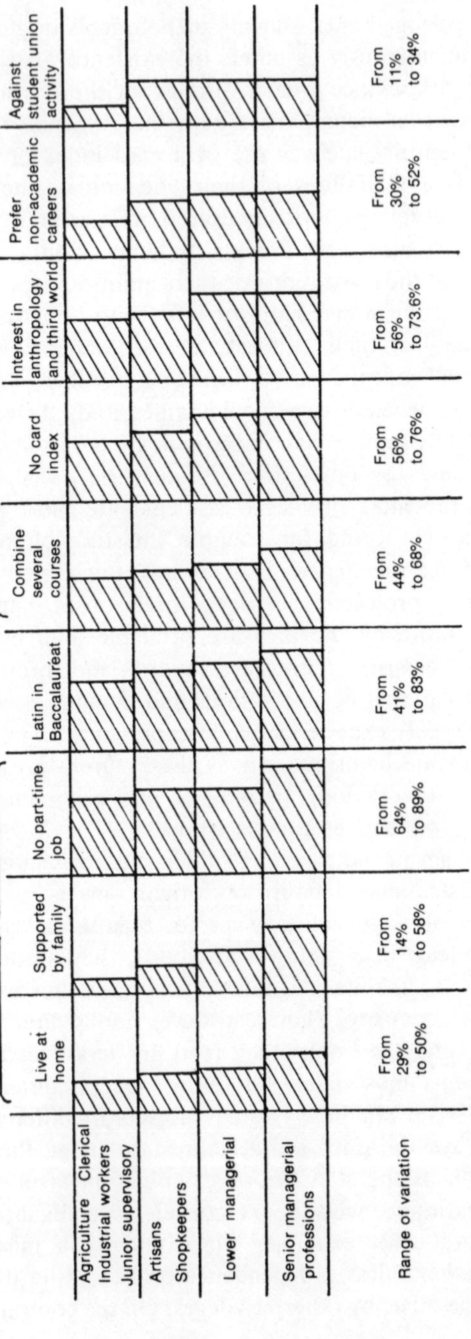

Fig. 3. Social Origin and Student Life

eclecticism enables them to make the most of the possibilities which the teaching offers. There is nothing to prevent a proportion (about one-third) of the privileged students from making an educational privilege out of what may constitute a disadvantage for the others, since, as we shall see, the university paradoxically most highly rewards the art of remaining aloof from "academic" values and disciplines.

Not only do the most privileged students derive from their background of origin habits, skills, and attitudes which serve them directly in their scholastic tasks, but they also inherit from it knowledge and know-how, tastes, and a "good taste" whose scholastic profitability is no less certain for being indirect. "Extra-curricular" culture (*la culture "libre"*), the implicit condition for academic success in certain disciplines, is very unequally distributed among students from different backgrounds, and inequality of income does not suffice to explain the disparities which we find. Cultural privilege is manifest when it is a matter of familiarity with works which only regular visits to theaters, galleries, and concerts can give (visits which the school does not organize, or only sporadically). It is still more manifest in the case of those works, generally the most modern ones, which are the least "scholastic."[13]

In every area of culture in which it is measured—be it the theater, music, painting, jazz, or the cinema—students have richer and more extensive knowledge the higher their social origin. While wide variation in the ability to play a musical instrument, in knowledge of plays through theater-going, or in knowledge of classical music through concert-going is in no way surprising, since class cultural habits and economic factors here combine their effects, it is remarkable that students diverge even more clearly, by social origin, in the frequency of their visits to museums and galleries, and even in their knowledge of the history of jazz or the cinema, which are often said to be "popular arts." When one discovers that in the case of painting, which is not directly taught, differences appear even in knowledge of the most classical artists and steadily increase for more modern painters, and that erudition about the cinema or jazz (always much rarer than for consecrated arts) is also very unequally distributed depending on social class, it has to be concluded that cultural inequalities are never more pronounced than in the area in which, in the absence of organized

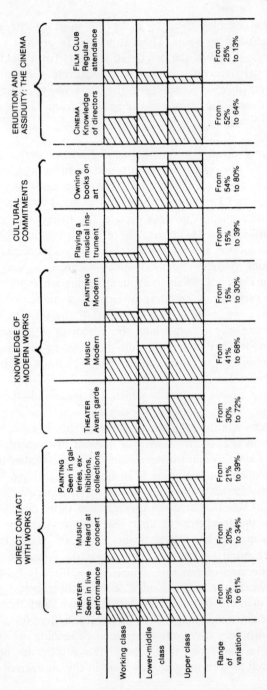

Fig. 4. Students' Social Origin and Aesthetic Activities

instruction, cultural behaviors obey social determinisms more than the logic of individual tastes and enthusiasms.[14]

Students from different backgrounds set themselves apart no less by the orientation of their aesthetic interests. To be sure, the social factors of differentiation may sometimes cancel out their most apparent effects, and petit-bourgeois seriousness can offset the advantage which upper-class students derive from familiarity with high culture. But the different values which orient similar behaviors may reveal themselves indirectly through more subtle differences. This is seen particularly clearly in the case of the theater, which, unlike painting or music, belongs both to the culture taught in school and to "extracurricular" culture. The sons of peasants, lower-rank executives, industrial workers, or senior executives may manifest an equivalent knowledge of classical drama, without having the same culture, even in this area, because they do not share the same cultural past. The same knowledge does not necessarily express the same attitudes or involve the same values. Whereas in one group it may testify to the exclusive power of scholastic rules and learning (since it has been largely acquired through independent or scholastically required reading rather than live performance), in another group, at least as much as obedience to scholastic imperatives, it expresses possession of a culture which these students owe first to their home background. Thus, when one uses a test or examination to draw up a table of tastes and knowledge at a given moment, one is cutting, at a determinate point, through all the different trajectories along which students have come to where they are.

Furthermore, a good knowledge of classical drama does not have the same significance among the children of Parisian senior executives, who combine it with a good knowledge of *avant-garde* theater and even middle-brow theater (*théâtre de boulevard*), as it does among the children of manual workers in Lille or Clermont-Ferrand, who have a similar knowledge of classical theater but know nothing of *avant-garde* or middle-brow theater. It is quite apparent that a purely scholastic culture is not simply a partial culture or a part of culture, but an inferior culture, because the very elements of which it is composed do not have the same significance they would have in a larger whole. The school system itself exalts a "general culture" diametrically opposed to what it denounces as the "scholastic" approach to culture in those whose social origins condemn them to have no other culture than the

one they have acquired at school. Every item of knowledge therefore has to be seen both as an element in a constellation and as a
moment in the cultural itinerary as a totality, in which each point
on the curve contains the whole curve. And, finally, it is the personal manner of performing cultural acts which gives them their
specifically cultural character: thus, ironic casualness, mannered
elegance, or the statutory assurance which lends ease or the af-
fectation of ease are almost always the mark of students from the
upper classes, where such manners signal membership in the elite.

Privilege is only noticed, most of the time, in its crudest forms
of operation—recommendations or connections, help with school-
work or extra teaching, information about education and employment. But, in fact, the essential part of a cultural heritage is
passed on more discretely and more indirectly, and even in the
absence of any methodical effort or overt action. It is perhaps in
the most "cultivated" backgrounds that there is least need to
preach devotion to culture or deliberately to undertake initiation
into cultural practices. In contrast to the petit-bourgeois milieu,
where most of the time the parents can only transmit cultural good
intentions, the cultivated classes contrive diffuse incitements that
are much more likely to induce espousal of culture through a sort
of hidden persuasion.

Thus, *lycée* pupils from the Paris bourgeoisie are able to manifest an extensive culture, acquired without intention or effort, as
if by osmosis, at the very moment when they are denying that
they experience the slightest parental pressure.

"Do you go to art galleries and museums?"
"Not very often. The school didn't often take us to art gal-
leries, more often it was history museums. My parents more often
take me to the theater. We don't go to galleries much."
"Who are your favorite painters?"
"Van Gogh, Braque, Picasso, Monet, Gauguin, and Cézanne.
I haven't seen the originals. I know them from books that I look
at at home. I play the piano from time to time. That's all. I prefer
listening to music to playing it. We have a lot of Bach, Mozart,
Schubert, and Schumann."
"Do your parents recommend books to you?"
"I read what I choose. We have lots of books. I take what I
want." (University teacher's daughter, age 13, Sèvres *lycée*.)
But though the differences between students in the area of
"general culture" always point back to social privileges or disad-

vantages, they do not always take the same form when they are considered in terms of teachers' expectations. The most culturally disadvantaged students may resort to more scholastic activities, such as reading plays, as a way of compensating for their handicap. Similarly, though knowledge of the cinema is distributed in accordance with the logic of privilege which gives students from well-off homes the taste and leisure to transfer cultivated habits into extracurricular areas, attendance at film clubs, a practice that is at once inexpensive, compensatory, and quasi-scholastic, seems to be most common among lower-middle-class students. For individuals from the most deprived backgrounds, the school remains the one and only path to culture, at every level of education. As such, it would be the royal road to the democratization of culture if it did not consecrate the initial cultural inequalities by ignoring them and if it did not—for example, by denigrating a piece of academic work as too "academic"—often devalue the culture it transmits, in favor of the inherited culture which does not bear the vulgar mark of effort and so has every appearance of ease and grace.

Differing through a whole set of predispositions and prior knowledge which they owe to their backgrounds, students are only *formally* equal in their acquisition of high culture. They are separated not by divergences which, each time, distinguish statistical categories differing in a different respect and for different reasons, but by systems of cultural features which (whether they acknowledge it or not) they share in part with their class of origin. The content and modality of their career plans, the type of scholastic behavior employed in the pursuit of that vocation, the most unconstrained directions of their artistic practice, in short, everything that defines the relation of a group of students to their studies, expresses the fundamental relation of a social class to the whole social structure, to social success, and to culture.[15]

All teaching, and more especially the teaching of culture (even scientific culture), implicitly presupposes a body of knowledge, skills, and, above all, modes of expression which constitute the heritage of the cultivated classes. Classical secondary schooling, an education *ad usum delphini*, conveys second-degree significations, taking for granted a whole treasury of first-degree experiences—books found in the family library, "choice" entertainments chosen by others, holidays organized as cultural pilgrimages, allusive conversations which only enlighten those already enlightened. It can only lead to a fundamental inequality in this game reserved for privileged persons, which all must enter because it presents itself to them adorned with the values of universality. If children from the disadvantaged classes often perceive scholastic initiation as an apprenticeship in artifice and in "language for teacher," is this not precisely because, for them, abstract reflexion has to precede direct experience? They have to learn in detail the layout of the Parthenon without ever having left their province, and to expatiate, throughout their schooling, with the same obligatory insincerity, on the *je ne sais quoi* and litotes of classical passion or the infinite, infinitesimal nuances of good taste. When people repeat that the content of traditional schooling takes away the reality of what it transmits, they forget to add that the sense of unreality is felt very unequally by students from different backgrounds.

Those who believe that everyone would be given equal access to the highest level of education and the highest culture, once the same economic means were provided for all those who have the requisite "gifts," have stopped halfway in their analysis of the obstacles; they ignore the fact that the abilities measured by scholastic criteria stem not so much from natural "gifts" (which must remain hypothetical so long as educational inequalities can be traced to other causes), but from the greater or lesser affinity between class cultural habits and the demands of the educational system or the criteria which define success within it. When pupils opt for the so-called cultural courses which always play a major role in determining their chances of a prestigious route through higher education (the Ecole Nationale d'Administration or Polytechnique, or the literature *agrégation*), they must assimilate a whole set of knowledge and techniques which are never completely separable from social values often contrary to those of their class of origin. For the children of peasants, manual workers, clerks, or small shopkeepers, the acquisition of culture is an acculturation.

These pupils themselves rarely experience their training as a renunciation and repudiation, because the knowledge they have to master is highly valued by society, and because this achievement symbolizes entry into the elite. Therefore, we must distinguish between ease in assimilating school-transmitted culture (which rises with social origin) and the propensity to acquire it, which is most intense among the petite bourgeoisie. Although the desire to rise socially by means of education may be no less great among the working classes than among the lower middle classes, it remains a fantasy, an abstraction, so long as there is only a minute objective likelihood of satisfying it. Manual workers may know nothing of the statistics which show that a manual worker's son has a less than 2 percent chance of going to college, but their behavior seems to be objectively adjusted in line with an empirical estimation of the objective chances which they share with all members of that category. This is why the petite bourgeoisie, the "transitional class," is the stratum most attached to scholastic values, because the educational system promises to answer all their aspirations by combining the values of social success with the values of cultural prestige. The members of the lower middle class set themselves apart from the working class by bestowing on elite culture—of which their practical knowledge is often equally remote—a conscious recognition which bears witness to their cultural good intentions, an empty determination to attain culture. Thus, students from the peasant and industrial working classes are doubly disadvantaged, both in terms of their facility in assimilating culture and their propensity to acquire it. Until recently, they did not even receive from their families encouragement to work hard at school, an encouragement which enables the lower middle class to make up for their dispossession by an aspiration to possess; and a continuous series of successes (as well as the repeated recommendation of the primary school teacher) used to be required in order for a child to be directed toward the *lycée*, a process which repeated itself at later stages in his education.

The reason why these and similar self-evident facts need to be restated is that the successes of a few too often cause it to be forgotten that they have only been able to overcome their cultural disadvantages by virtue of exceptional abilities and certain exceptional features of their family backgrounds. Since university entrance presupposes in some cases a unbroken run of "miracles" and efforts, the relative equality between students selected with very unequal severity may conceal the inequalities on which it is based.

Even if academic success were achieved by lower-middle-class students as often as by students from the cultivated classes, the two groups would still be set apart by subtle differences in their approach to culture. It cannot be ruled out that the teacher who contrasts the "brilliant" or "gifted" pupil with the "earnest" or "hardworking" pupil is, in a good many cases, judging nothing other than the relation to culture to which each is socially assigned by birth. The petit-bourgeois student, who tends to commit himself unreservedly to classroom learning and to involve in his work the occupational virtues valued by his milieu (for example, the cult of work performed with rigor and difficulty), will be judged by the criteria of the cultivated elite, which many teachers readily make their own, even and especially when their membership in the "elite" dates from their entry into the teaching profession. The aristocratic image of culture and intellectual work has such close similarities to the most widespread representation of accomplished culture that it imposes itself even on those minds least suspected of indulgence toward theories of the elite, preventing them from going beyond the call for formal equality.

The reversal of the scale of values which, by inverting the signs, transforms seriousness into the "spirit of seriousness" and the valuing of work into a trivial, laborious pedantry suspected of making up for a lack of talent, takes place as soon as the petit-bourgeois ethos is judged from the standpoint of the ethos of the "elite," that is, measured against the dilettantism of the cultivated, well-born gentleman who knows without having struggled to acquire his knowledge and who, secure about his present and future, can afford detachment and risk virtuosity. But the culture of the elite is so close to the culture taught in school that a child from a petit-bourgeois background (and *a fortiori* from a peasant or working-class background) can only laboriously acquire that which is given to a child from the cultivated class—style, taste, sensibility, in short, the savoir-faire and art of living that are natural to a class because they are the culture of that class.[16] For some, the learning of elite culture is a conquest paid for in effort; for others, it is a heritage, which implies both facility and the temptations of facility.

Social advantages or disadvantages weigh so heavily on educational careers and, more generally, on all cultural life, because, perceived or unperceived, they are always cumulative. For example, the father's position in the social hierarchy is strongly linked to a similar position for other members of the family, and is not independent of the chances of going to secondary school in a city or a small town, which are known to be significantly linked to unequal degrees of knowledge and practice of the arts. This is just one of the more remote manifestations of the influence of the geographical factor, which first determines the clear-cut inequalities in the chances of entering secondary and higher education: the rate of enrollment ranges from less than 20 percent to more than 60 percent, depending on the *département,* for the 11 to 17 age group; and from less than 2 percent to 10 percent for the 19 to 24 age group; these differences depend both on the proportion of the active population employed in farming and on the density of population. In fact, the geographical factor and the social factor in social inequality are never independent, since, as we have seen, the chances of living in a city, where there is more likelihood of access to education and culture, rise with position in the social hierarchy. Thus, as regards knowledge of the arts, the sharpest contrast is between the children and grandchildren of senior executives, brought up in Paris, and the children and grandchildren of farm workers, brought up in centers of less than 50,000 inhabitants.

Thus, though ignored or denied, the influence of social factors is at work in the student milieu, but not in the form of a mechanical determinism. For example, it would be a mistake to suppose that cultural heritage favors all its recipients automatically and similarly. We have, in fact, seen at least two ways of relating to privilege and two types of operation of privilege. Inheritance always implies the danger of squandering the heritage, especially when it consists of culture, that is, an acquisition in which the manner of acquiring it is part of its essence. When a cultural heritage is invested in the superficial pastime of elegant parlor games, it does not produce, to the same degree and at the different levels of education, the scholastic profit that students from the lower classes derive from their forced inclination to concentrate on the most reliable investments. But, used rationally, a cultural heritage favors educational success, without confining its holder to the more or less narrow interests defined by the school system; those who belong to a cultivated milieu which is aware of the real intellectual or scientific hierarchies are able to relativize the educational influences which exercise too much authority or prestige on others. It would be easy to demonstrate in the same way that although subjects from the most disadvantaged classes are those most likely to be crushed by the weight of their social destiny, they can also, exceptionally, turn their excessive handicap into the stimulus they need to overcome it. Would the sons of workers or petit-bourgeois who have made it to higher education evince so strongly and so generally the energy of a Julien Sorel or the ambition of a Rastignac if this were not precisely what had enabled these students to avoid the common fate of their class?

There is a need for more detailed study of the causes or reasons which govern these exceptional destinies, but everything suggests that they would be found in some special feature of family background. Given that, as we have seen, the objective chances of university entrance are *forty times* greater for a senior executive's son than for a worker's son, a survey might be expected to show approximately the same ratio between the average number of individuals having been to university in working-class and in senior-executive families. But we find that, among a group of medical students, the average number of members of the extended family who are or have been in higher education varies in the ratio of only *one to four* between working-class students and upper-class students.[17] Thus, students from the disadvantaged strata who enter university differ profoundly, in this respect at least, from the other individuals of their category. The presence in the family circle of a relative who is or has been in higher education is evidence that these families are in an unusual cultural situation, if only in that they offer a greater subjective expectation of university entrance. This would have to be confirmed empirically, but it may be supposed that it is their relative unawareness of their disadvantage (based on an intuitive assessment of their educational chances) that frees these subjects from one of the most real disadvantages of their category, namely, the resigned renunciation of "impossible" ambitions. If students from the working classes are, in fact, drawn from the least disadvantaged strata of the most disadvantaged classes, this would explain why the working-class representation in education tends to stabilize once this marginal category has been taken up. For example, after having increased regularly, the proportion of industrial workers' sons in secondary education has now leveled out at about 15 percent.

If privileges as different in kind as living in Paris or belonging to the cultured class are almost always associated with the same attitude toward education and culture, this is because they are in practice connected and because they favor adherence to values whose common root is nothing other than the fact of privilege. The weight of cultural heredity is such that it is here possible to possess exclusively without even having to exclude others, since everything takes place as if the only people excluded were those who excluded themselves. The relation which the subjects have to their class condition and to the social determinisms which define it is part of the complete definition of their condition and of the conditionings which it imposes. These determinisms do not need to be consciously perceived in order to force subjects to take their decisions in terms of them, in other words, in terms of the *objective future* of their social category. It may even be, in a more general way, that the determinisms are that much more rigorous in their influence when the extent of their influence is less clearly recognized.

This is why the most effective way of serving the system while believing one is fighting it is to attribute all inequalities in educational opportunity solely to economic inequalities or to a conscious political aim. The educational system can, in fact, ensure the perpetuation of privilege by the mere operation of its own internal logic. It follows that any demand for reform which isolates one aspect of the educational system, whether higher education as a whole, or, by a second-degree abstraction, this or that aspect of higher education, objectively serves the system and all that the system serves, since one only has to let these factors take their course, from infants' school through to higher education, in order to ensure the perpetuation of social privilege. Thus, the mechanisms which ensure the elimination of working-class and lower-middle-class children would operate almost as efficiently (but more discreetly) in a situation in which a systematic policy of providing scholarships or grants made subjects from all social classes formally equal vis-à-vis education. It would then be possible, with more justification than ever, to invoke unequal giftedness or unequal cultural aspirations to explain the unequal representation of the different social strata in the different levels of education.

In short, the potency of the social factors of inequality is such that even if the equalization of economic resources could be achieved, the university system would not cease to consecrate inequalities by transforming social privilege into individual gifts or merits. Rather, if formal equality of opportunity were achieved, the school system would be able to employ all the appearances of legitimacy in its work of legitimating privileges.

2.Games Students Play

I<small>N A SORT OF HUMOROUS SERMON WHICH HE</small>
probably delivered to the pupils of his college, Robert de Sorbon
did not hesitate to compare the Arts faculty examination to the
Last Judgment and even went so far as to say that the university
judges were much more severe than the judges in Heaven. . . .

At Bologna only Law was taught. The law students were
middle-aged men, often clergymen who already held livings. Such
audiences had no intention of being dictated to, so they formed
a corporation, a *Universitas*, distinct from and independent
of the masters' college. And, by virtue of its strong organization,
their corporation was able to lay down the law and impose its
will on the teachers, who were forced to go along with whatever
their pupils wanted. This may strike you as a paradoxical kind
of academic organization, but it has existed and in more
cases than one.

Durkheim, L'évolution pédagogique en France.

Educational inequalities most often remain unnoticed and are
always what is least mentioned when students are discussed and
especially when students talk about themselves. But they are
sufficiently visible, at least as regards their strictly economic aspect,
to make it necessary to look for the unity of the student world in
identical university practice rather than in identical conditions of
existence. Acceptance of the same rules of university law, com-
pliance with the same administrative formalities (enrollment,
health checks, and so on), coping *en masse* with inadequate
premises, anonymous lecture theaters or examination halls, queue-
ing together to get into the refectory or library, suffering the constraints of the same syllabus or the idiosyncrasies of the same
teachers, writing essays on the same subjects or confronting the
same lecture topics—is all that sufficient to define, even in vague

or negative terms, an integrated group and an occupational situation?

It is true that, in general, analysis of the specific features of the occupational activity, the social organization in which it is carried on, its rhythms, its tools, and the constraints they impose, is a *sine qua non* for any understanding of the behavior, attitudes, and ideologies of an occupational body. However, a group in constant flux, whose members differ as much in terms of their social past as of their occupational future and who, up to now at least, do not experience their occupational training as itself an occupation, are likely to require definition in terms of the meaning and symbolic function they almost unanimously confer on their practice, rather than in terms of the unity of their practice.

Students certainly live and mean to live in a special time and space. Their studenthood momentarily frees them from family life and working life. Encapsulated in the autonomy of university time, they escape, even more completely than their teachers, from the schedules of society at large, knowing no other deadline than the *dies irae* of the examination and no other timetable than the undemanding pattern of weekly lectures. The academic faith has its regular communicants and its seasonal attenders, but all of them, whatever their rate of observance, live in the rhythm of the university year. The only calendar imposed derives its structure from the cycle of study. With its high points—the effervescence of registration and the feverishness on the eve of examinations—framing the long, low-key treck through the year, when attendance flags and new-year resolutions founder, the university year establishes the rhythm for academic effort and intellectual adventure, structures experience and memory around successes and failures, and tailors ambitions to the scope of its narrow horizon.

Aside from the constraints imposed by this calendar, there are neither dates nor schedules. The student situation enables the temporal frameworks of social life to be broken, or their priorities reversed. Realizing one is a student means first, and perhaps foremost, feeling free to go to the movies at any time and therefore never on a Sunday when other people do; contriving to weaken or reverse the major oppositions which imperiously organize adults' work and leisure; flouting the distinction between weekends and weekdays, day and night, work time and playtime.

More generally, the student tends to break up all the oppositions
which structure life by subjecting it to constraints, such as those
which separate idle chatter from organized, purposeful discussion,
hobbies from academic culture, educational exercises from personal creativity.

> "It's the only time in life when you can put off what you've
> got to do, work when it suits you, be unemployed if you
> feel like it . . ." (senior executive's son, Paris, age 26).
> "Being a student means working when you want to, having
> time to take an interest in things, more leisure, elastic time"
> (senior executive's son, Paris, 23). "There's no such thing
> as leisure; I refuse to draw a line between work and leisure, I
> don't accept that dichotomy. Either it's arbitrary or it's a
> confession of failure by people whose work bores them"
> (junior executive's son, Paris). "My work isn't unpleasant; it's
> not something I'm forced to do. I could almost say all my
> work is leisure; I'm glad to be working because I'm lucky
> enough not to be obliged to do it" (junior executive's son,
> Paris). "During the year, for me work is a sort of leisure and
> leisure is a sort of work; they just overlap, and I think I
> tend to go for leisure more than work, anyway, I have the
> impression, subjectively, that student life has a lot more
> leisure than work in it, if you take work to mean something
> arduous or unpleasant. Work, the Kantian notion of duty,
> has never appealed to me much, and I think I'd rather do
> nothing at all than . . . Still, all the same, you've got to do
> a modicum of work, you've got to make a little bit of an
> effort" (senior executive's son, Paris). "I don't often see it as
> a problem, especially as far as timetables are concerned.
> I don't separate work and leisure. If there's a decent movie on,
> I go and see it, whether it's a weekday or a Sunday. The
> question really doesn't arise. There's no particular pattern
> to my leisure activities; I choose what I'm going to do but I
> don't organize it. I choose according to what comes up,
> rather than drawing up a calendar. I don't have season tickets
> anywhere, and there are no fixed or regular dates for seeing
> people. . . . I don't have any set habits for leisure time. . . .
> There's nothing fixed. Since I live at home, there are no set
> periods for leisure, as such, but it must add up to quite a
> number of hours" (senior executive's daughter, Paris).

However factitious and superficial, these freedoms are the conscious liberties by which the "fresher" persuades himself he has

become a student. The novice may take a long time to acquire the art of organizing his own work; but, because everything inclines him to do so, he will immediately and totally adopt the life-style defined by the most prestigious intellectual models.

"Yes, I waste a terrible amount of time; I don't know how to organize my work properly, and since work has to come before leisure—that's only right and proper—I have no time left for leisure . . ." (senior executive's son, Paris). "When I don't want to work any longer, and I'm sitting at a table, I plan what I'm going to do during the week. . . . I try to work out a timetable so in theory I know what I've got to do with my time. In theory, but, of course, depending on the weather and the mood I'm in, either it works or it doesn't" (senior executive's son, Paris). "My problem, if you like, is one of organization. . . . The fact is, I don't seem able to discipline myself, it's always the same story. . . . I have the most appalling difficulty in accepting any discipline, any plan of work" (senior executive's son, Paris). "I think the problem lies at the level of mental organization, there's something that doesn't quite click, that I haven't yet managed to coordinate. I have trouble seeing what the order of priorities ought to be. For example, if there's something that needs doing around the house, I get up to go and do it, and, just as I'm getting up, I realize there's something else that needs doing; it's just one distraction after another. . . . I suffer for it. I still have thirty books to read for my degree, and every day I pick up a different one. Every day? Every hour, more likely. I tell myself I've got to read this, then I pick up a book and read three or four pages and then in the evening something else catches my eye and I pick up another one" (shopkeeper's son, Paris).

This libertarian use of "free" time may be a specifically student characteristic, but it does not supply a positive definition of the student condition. Unlike the social rhythms which make integrated groups by subjecting everyone's activities to the same constraints, the unstructured chronology of university life brings students together only negatively, because their individual rhythms may have nothing in common beyond their different ways of differing from the major collective rhythms.

Doubtless, wherever university life has developed, it has marked out the landscape with its dwelling places, its customary haunts, and necessary routes between them. Its residential and leisure zones, even when scattered throughout the city, have a specific character to which ordinary language bears witness: there are "student" neighborhoods, "student" cafés, "student" rooms. But, quite apart from the fact that most students have nothing in common beyond attending the same lectures, it is impossible to credit the mere fact of coexistence or coresidence with the power to make a coherent group out of the individuals which they juxtapose. It is not space as such, but a regulated, temporally structured use of space that gives a group a framework for integration.

This can be seen in the different consequences of residence in university halls and in traditional boarding institutions. The preparatory classes for the *grandes écoles* (and consequently, though to a lesser extent, the *grandes écoles* themselves) represent islands of integration, where one finds a body of oral or written traditions, initiation rites, and rites of passage, a code governing interpersonal relations which presupposes a hierarchy based on seniority, a slang which serves to name what is most specific about the experience, and a "cast of mind" which enables their alumni to be recognized and to recognize each other throughout their lives. The reason for this is that, here, daily rhythms and the temporal distribution of tasks take on their full structuring power by virtue of the organization of activities that is imposed by school discipline. As in the traditional village, regulated activities and the contacts imposed and multiplied by the uniformity of the rule enable everyone to know everything about everyone without recourse to direct experience. Not that we would offer this type of forced, total integration as an ideal for relations between fellow students, or even as a model of efficient work; rather, our intention is to show, by means of this limiting case, that a common space and time are integrative factors only when their use is regulated by an institution or a tradition.

The grouping of university activities in a single space, the campus, is sometimes expected to produce a complete transformation of all social relationships, whether between students and teachers or among the students. In reality, while separate living space is bound to create the negative conditions of integration, intensified collective activities, especially cooperative activities, in the absence of the traditional machinery of community integration, presuppose an institution and a specialized personnel charged with organizing collective work and teaching the techniques of cooperation. And, indeed, signs of integration only appear in the student world when a group is required by an existing institution to organize itself, or when cooperation is imposed by the scholastic imperatives of learning, for example, as far as the Arts faculties are concerned, in certain specialized institutes.

But the ideal of cooperation finds no encouragement in the French university tradition and, from primary school to scientific research, collective work can only exceptionally be based on institutions. Among the tasks they set themselves, teachers often give the lowest priority to the organizing function which might befall them, in particular, the task of establishing the framework for students' collective work. Furthermore, from early childhood, the school system inculcates a contrary ideal, that of individualistic competition. Therefore, students may well have a hankering for team work to contrast with the reality of the university, but, being products of the system, they are in no way prepared for inventing techniques that would go against values they have internalized years earlier. Thus, the frequent failure of university working groups stems, above all, from the fact that, as products of a system which develops the inclination toward passivity, students would need a quasi-miraculous determination to be able to create new forms of integration *ex nihilo*.

And the traditions which, symbolically at least, used to integrate the student world of the past, have crumbled away and are now the preserve of marginal groups. Student folklore, with its processions and songs, has lasted longest in small provincial university towns, and testifies to integration into the local community rather than into the student world. Such signs of specificity were most marked in periods when the student population represented nothing other than an age group and when "education" provided well-to-do young gentlemen with a respite or transition ritually inserted at the threshold of a bourgeois career. Faculties such as Law or Medicine, perhaps because they have remained the most bourgeois, or because they lead into more traditional professional bodies, are today the last bastions of the rituals of incorporation. But, in relative terms, their student numbers have regularly and markedly declined, and so they no longer set the tone of university life.

Law and medical students, who accounted for 60 percent of the student population at the turn of the century, now represent less than 30 percent, whereas Science and Arts students make up 65 percent of the total compared to less than 25 percent in 1901. Such a reversal was bound to produce qualitative changes, both in the image which outside groups have of students and in students' images of each other. Today's *modal* student is no longer a law or medical student, a fact which is not without significance when one thinks of the type of attitude favored by the more bourgeois recruitment and the professional outlets of those two faculties.[1]

Deprived of institutional supports and social frameworks, increasingly distant from the obsolete traditions of student life, the student milieu is perhaps less integrated today than ever before. One does not even find there the play of formal oppositions between subgroups, a game which provides a minimum of integration in groupings as ephemeral and artificial as the *lycée* or primary school. The distinction between Arts and Science students or, within a given faculty, between different disciplines and different years, is purely administrative; seniority or type of studies only ever give rise to statistical categories. The absence of reciprocal stereotypes or of joking relationships bears witness to the lack of *esprit de corps* and the rarity of contacts and exchanges. Similarly, rather than genuine argots, one only finds a lingua franca made up various argots, borrowed from various sources and incapable of defining membership of a group, even by exclusion. Finally, the degree of mutual acquaintance among fellow-students (and *a fortiori* students in different disciplines) is very low, especially in Paris. Exchanges are, naturally, most frequent among the students who attend most regularly and who are, it would appear, those most dependent on the teaching given; but the only networks of acquaintance which have any continuity or consistence are those which date from previous schooling or which are based on external social ties, such as geographical origin, religious or political affiliation, and especially membership in the most well-to-do social classes.

All the sociometric tests show that exchanges outside the classroom, and even knowing other students' names, are extremely rare. If, as various indices suggest, the most sustained and varied exchanges are those among upper-class students, this is, no doubt, as countless other details testify, because they are more at ease in the university milieu and also, perhaps, because their previous education has equipped them with techniques of sociability appropriate to such an environment. A small-scale survey in Lille suggests that, other things being equal, male and female students from the wealthiest classes are those best known to their fellow-students and, although to a lesser extent, those who know most of them. Similarly, since the fact of sitting close to the professorial dais can be regarded as a sign of ease and self-assurance, it is not surprising that, whatever the degree of acquaintance considered (from knowing by sight to working together), the number of fellow-students known declines steadily as one moves from the front rows to the back rows of the amphitheater.[2]

This weak integration is doubtless an obstacle to the transmission of technical information and intellectual stimulation. Thus, among the students using Lille University library, three times as many say they have read or borrowed books on the advice of a lecturer as have done so on the advice of a friend. Similarly, the influence of friends only rarely plays a part in the choice of a course or a career. But sporadic contacts and chance conversations are nonetheless sufficient to propagate rumors, often wild ones, about teachers and their idiosyncratic demands. Whereas information about examinations percolates slowly and uncertainly (there are always a large number of students who turn up for exams knowing nothing of the possible options or the duration of the tests), the most extravagant tales spread like wildfire. This is how most myths about examinations or examiners come into being. Such rumor-mongering can favor cultural contagion or imitation without genuinely integrating the mass of students into common values, just as it can sustain the ideal of genuine integration, or nostalgia for it, without providing the means of achieving it. As soon as the aim arises of organizing exchanges for practical ends, for example, setting up effective work groups, the absence of institutional or traditional mechanisms of integration is remorselessly underlined.

Thus, everything leads one to doubt whether students really constitute a homogeneous, independent, and integrated social group. While it is true that the student situation contains enough specific characteristics to justify our endeavor, at one level of analysis, to relate to that situation the attitudes most directly connected with it, the fact remains that complete autonomization of the student milieu would make a sociological approach to it impossible. The sociology of a group whose members have only their university practice in common and who are differentiated in countless ways, even in that practice, by their social origin, can only be a *particular case* (whose particularity, of course, needs to be defined) of the sociology of social inequalities vis-à-vis the educational system and the culture it transmits.

More akin to a fluid aggregate than an occupational group, the student world would present all the symptoms of anomie if students were only students and were not integrated into other groups, that is, in most cases, their families or, secondarily, elective groupings such as religious associations or political parties. But since, despite their appearance or their names, these are organizations *for* students much more than student organizations, those who remain students sufficiently to experience lack of integration in the form of solitude or neglect find that organizations which begin to give some reality to the ideal of an integrated milieu only makes them feel more strongly their nostalgia for integration. Thus, female students, who are more tied to their families or to secondary associations, are also those who initiate most of the attempts to animate fellow students. But the well-meaning voluntarism of these endeavors is sufficient to show that they can neither draw on a living tradition of festive techniques nor on any sense of community.

Every year, among the philosophy students in a provincial Arts faculty, there are attempts to organize collective activities, which regularly fail, no doubt because they come up against the aristocratic individualism of the "philosophers." These sporadic efforts at organization are the work of those who cannot or will not sublimate their solitude into the ideal of solitary meditation, that is, first and foremost, girls who transpose the task of organizing exchanges, which is characteristic of woman's traditional role, into their university role. In 1964, the student board of the Institute consisted of five women and one man (a member of the "*Corpo*"[3] and chairman of the philosophers' "Catholic Group"). Although the active nucleus of the Institute consisted of members of the "student parish," although three quarters of the Social Science and Philosophy students declared themselves to be Catholics, and although the "Catholic Group" included twenty-five Philosophy students among its members, the only events which met with any success were those in which faculty staff also took part: a meal (forty-five participants, half of them men) and a cultural excursion to Paris (twenty-five participants). In all the other cases, a dinner without the lecturers and a "pancake party," the group was reduced to the nucleus of Catholic activists, with a majority of women each time. The plan to review together for the examinations never got beyond the stage of pious intentions.

In Paris, where the student milieu is less integrated than anywhere else, such conpensatory behavior is even rarer, and the resignation of the majority coexists with the ideological yearnings of a few. Whereas contact with teachers is naturally much rarer in Paris than in the provinces, it is demanded less often in Paris, at least by the mass of students, perhaps because reality exposes more clearly the unreality of such an aspiration. On the other hand, provincial students can call for an intensification of exchanges which seem to them to be prevented by university habits rather than precluded by material necessities.

Thus, everything takes place as if, below a certain threshold, reasonable expectations, too manifestly belied and refuted by reality, had to give way to resignation or utopianism. It is doubtless no accident that Paris students, condemned by the present system to mere spatial coexistence, passive attendance, and solitary competition for qualifications, crushed by the experience of anonymity and the diffuse aggression of crowds, tend to abandon realistic criticism of reality in favor of the conceptual terrorism of verbal demands which are, to a large extent, satisfied merely by being formulated. The utopian belief that "small work groups" could produce more intensive communication between students only by detaching them completely from the grip of the university organization, and the myth of totally nondirective teaching, mutual education, and collective Socraticism, merely project the need for integration in the form of the formal ideal of integration for integration's sake.

However unrealistic they may be, the most exaggerated formulations of this ideology must be taken seriously, because it may be that they express one of the truths that the student milieu is most careful to hide from itself. Perhaps it would not be going too far to wonder whether the most extremist ideology does not express the *objective truth* of a group dominated by values and habits of thought which it owes to its bourgeois recruitment, its Parisian base, and the more traditionalist character of its university speciality.

However different they may be, however great the inequalities between their living conditions and their chances of success, students at least have in common the desire to achieve, both in the

myth of unity and in the game of diversification, individual iden-
tification with something which, without being a model, is less
than an ideal and more than a stereotype, and which defines a
historical essence of the student. The endeavor to understand some
of the deep-rooted attitudes of students in terms of the generic
forms of the student situation is justified, inasmuch as this situation contains, as an objective possibility, the temptation of a relation to studenthood and to education which is valid as a historical
type, even if it is very unequally actualized by the various categories of students.

If it is futile to hope to find specifically student models of behavior underlying sporadic, fluctuating conformisms, whether vesti-
mentary, cosmetic, or ideological, this is perhaps because students
resemble one another mainly through the nature of their relation
to what they are and what they do, or, more precisely, through
the meaning they give to what they are and what they do. If the
behaviors by which the observer generally recognizes a student are
first and foremost symbolic behaviors, that is, acts by which he
bears witness before others and before himself to his capacity to
present an original image of the student, this is because he is condemned by his transitional, preparatory position to be only what
he has the project of being, or even to be a pure project for being.

This project does not predetermine the content of the symbolic
behaviors in which it is enacted in any univocal way. The sometimes assiduous and methodical will to achieve full studenthood
does not presuppose unanimous recognition of an image of the
ideal student, since the image of what one seeks to actualize may
amount to no more than the imperative urge to actualize an
image. To want to be, and to want to choose one's identity, is,
first of all, to refuse to be what one has not chosen to be. The
first necessity that is refused or transfigured is that of being rooted
in a social milieu. Students generally evade the simple naming of
their parents' occupation, whatever it may be. Their embarrassed
silence, half-truths, or declared dissociation are all ways of distancing themselves from the unacceptable idea that such an un-
chosen determination could determine the choices of someone
entirely occupied in choosing what he is to be.[4] The aspiration to
create and choose oneself does not impose a determinate behavior,
but only a symbolic use of behavior intended to signify that this
behavior has been chosen. So the affirmations or denegations that
run interchangeably through the student's discourse about students

and about himself qua student always return to the question that constitutes his being, the question of what he is.

> "I never think of myself as a student" (architecture student, female, age 20). "There isn't just 'a student'; you're not *just* a student" (sociology student, female, 20). "I'm a student the same way I'm other things too" (psychology student, female, 27). "The student is *me*; if you ask me questions I can only talk about myself" (sociology student, male, 21).

As soon as any behavior (whether wearing a pea jacket or admiring Cannonball Adderly) is asserted with a regularity or frequency that condemns it to banality, it surrenders its differentiating power to the conduct which refuses it. To distinguish oneself as a student means, in fact, to distinguish oneself from the student essence in which one encapsulates others.

> 'I'm a special case, I don't correspond to what people call a student" (archeology student, female, 20). "I'm not a student" (psychology student, male, 26). "The archetypal student is the independent student . . . There's a fashion, there are intellectual trends, but they're mostly followed by those who want to cultivate a student style" (sociology student, male, 24). "The image ,of the sort of student who hangs around the Sorbonne: he looks miserable, he walks around with *Le Monde* under his arm, he sits talking in cafés . . . he complains about the Sorbonne because people aren't happy there . . ." (anthropology student, female, 21).

Every relation to any constraint, of whatever nature, tends to be enacted here in terms of the symbolic transfiguration of necessity into freedom. If space and time are experienced in the most unreal way possible, this is because students symbolically reinterpret these constraints in order to choose, within them, to *be* students. Certain places may be frequented exclusively by students, such as university restaurants, or mainly so, such as certain cafés, and yet still not create a social bond between the small groups which are juxtaposed within them. Unlike the working-class café, where the exchanges involve all the "regulars," the elementary unit in student cafés remains the company around a table, because a good number of students are there essentially to consume the symbolic meanings invested in the café and in solitary work in the café. Far from setting itself and its users in a space designated for communication or cooperation, the café—like the film club or jazz cellar—belongs to a mythic space where students come and meet the archetypal student more than they meet each other. Even the student boarding house room, a space imposed by economic constraints, can lend itself to the play of symbolic transfigurations. In contrast to the rented room in a private home or in a student residence, it takes its place, even for those who lament being reduced to it, in a literary space which privileges opposing extremes, the high and the low, the garret and the cellar, and by its very poverty, it manifests the risks of a vocation and the price of freedom.

Students are particularly irreducible to their class of origin and even to their situation and their practice (which are always closely linked to their origin) because, as intellectual apprentices, they are defined by their *relation* to their class of origin, their situation, and their practice and, as aspiring intellectuals, they strive to live out this relation according to the models of the intellectual class, reinterpreted in terms of their own situation. In reaction against the disciplines of secondary school, the student asserts his identity as the subject of a cultural free will, frequenting the film club, buying records and a record player, decorating his room with prints, discovering the literary or cinematic avant-garde. Whether in political and cultural discussions or in the borrowing of books and records, the exchanges are not always sufficiently informed for it to be possible to speak of mutual education, but they seem at least to have the effect of favoring the recognition of cultural values. Older converts act as intercessors and intermediaries, leading the neophytes into an obligatory adherence to a cultural universe which might otherwise appear as the preserve of adults or mandarins.

As an adolescent and an apprentice, the student, more than anyone else, looks for guides to orient his thinking and his lifestyle. He is therefore particularly susceptible to the prestige of the examples which, as a future intellectual, he can only seek in the intellectual world; and, often enough, in that section of the intellectual world with which his daily practice brings him into direct and permanent contact, in other words, his university teachers. A group defined by its aspiration to culture naturally favors belief in cultural values and in the value of those who transmit or embody them. And it may well be that one or another of his teachers, directly encountered, will present the prestigious image of the intellectual that the student aspires to become. Every student's academic path is crossed by some "great professor," and it is always in the name of a prestigious *maître à penser* that the routine of mere pedagogues is rejected. By splitting the professorial *imago* in two, the student is able to identify with the values embodied in the "good teacher," in spite of his aversion to tyrannical, repetitive, or boring teachers. The teacher can even appear as the guarantor and sanction of those commitments that are furthest from the world of education: there is a sort of perfection, and an attendant beatitude, in serving the same political causes as one's intellectual master.

It may be objected—the argument is a fashionable one—that teachers' influence is nothing compared to the competing influences, such as the modern media, that are better designed to satisfy contemporary expectations. It would be easy to demonstrate that, at least in the student world, the university remains the major vehicle of the most traditional culture, and also, indirectly and secondarily, of the less orthodox cultural contents. For example, experts on cinema or jazz are much rarer than critics carried away by their professional interest would like to think—infinitely rarer, in any case, than experts on those arts on which there are university courses. And above all, the students who score best in these fields are the ones who are best adapted to the university and can transpose their scholastic techniques and interests.

Far from constituting a parallel, alternative, or compensatory culture, knowledge of cinema or jazz varies in direct proportion to familiarity with the traditional arts. It is natural, therefore, that the groups most integrated into the academic universe, and at the highest levels, should have the best scores in jazz and cinema as well as in other fields. For example, when asked to name the directors of a number of films, 94 percent of the Polytechnique students were able to supply at least one name, compared to only 69 percent of the faculty students; similarly, 73 percent of the *polytechniciens* showed an elementary knowledge of jazz, as against only 49 percent of the faculty students.

Specifically student cultural enterprises, such as theater groups or poetry clubs are, as is well known, rare phenomena, and they only keep going when they are based on university institutions or correspond to scholastic demands. Thus, in the Sorbonne, the Greek Theater group and the modern drama group have only been kept up and developed thanks to a slide into a quasi-professionalism that is perceived as such by most students, who only attend their productions when the plays are on the syllabus.

Because, in their declared opinions or superficial attitudes, students like to question the efficacy of educational action, and because people want to prove to themselves that teaching no longer influences anything or anybody, it is often forgotten that teaching largely succeeds in arousing in its pupils the need for the products it dispenses. The teacher always has the task of creating the propensity to consume knowledge, as well as the task of satisfying it. The traditional French university is perhaps the system in which the influence of teaching on the cultural goods market is most clearly visible. Professorial charisma is a permanent incitement to cultivated consumption: the display of virtuosity, the play of laudatory allusions or depreciatory silences, are sufficient to orient the student's practice, often decisively. It it often ironically remarked that many a student has taken himself for a "philosopher" because he has had a prestigious philosophy teacher, but it is less often seen that teachers' influence also extends to areas that are not directly taught.[5]

Student and teacher, products of the system, express the logic of the system. The student in no way contributes toward orienting the "production" or transmission of knowledge; the teacher never (or hardly ever) consults the student about his needs, and, when he tries to do so, he generally encounters passivity or amazement on the part of the student, who, filled with an undifferentiated propensity to absorb knowledge, precisely expects the teacher to indicate his priorities and to choose to satisfy the needs that he has created by deciding to satisfy them. Thus, everything is left to the teacher: it is up to him to define the syllabuses, the contents of the lectures, written work, and reading, as well as the amount of frivolity that can safely be injected into the educational machine. In the present state of the system, study of consumption can be collapsed into study of production: to know what the student (and, *a fortiori*, the *lycée* pupil) consumes, it is sufficient (or virtually so) to know what the teaching produces. Booksellers in small towns are well aware of this: before stocking up on Marx rather than Nietzsche, they wait for the new philosophy teacher to show his colors. Philosophy teachers in *lycées* play a key role in the scholastic consecration of novelties: with a course on Heidegger, by making room for Sartre or cybernetics rather than Mauriac or euthanasia, they decree (for their forty pupils a year) the cultural needs which are honorable and those which are not.

It is not surprising, then, that year in, year out, the educational industry manages to turn out a particularly homogeneous batch of consumers. To be convinced of this, one only has to consider the cultural orthodoxy exemplified in those exhibition products, the winners of the *Concours Général*.[6] In 1963, of the eighteen first-prize winners (of whom fifteen were the children of senior executives or members of the professions and three the sons of shopkeepers), thirteen said they intended to go into teaching or research, thereby expressing their appreciation of a university system that had appreciated them at their true worth. All of them gave reading as their favorite pastime, and their preferred authors all belonged to the small circle of the consecrated avant-garde of the time: Camus, Malraux, Valéry, Kafka, Proust. Eleven said they particularly liked classical music and the theater; cinema and jazz achieved only second place. They indignantly repudiated the idea that Johnny Hallyday represented modern youth, and they put Greece at the top of the list of the countries they would like to visit. Thus, every year, in their plans for the future, the young prizewinners reveal the same virtues that are celebrated in obituaries. Considering the winners of the first prize in philosophy, French, or classics as the most accomplished realization of the values attached to classical education, we can compose the ideal type of *homo academicus* in his juvenile form: the philosophy prizewinner in 1964 was the son and grandson of teachers, and intended to aim for the Ecole Normale Supérieure, take the *agrégation* there, and become a philosophy teacher; while the winner of the first prize in Latin translation had "read the whole of French literature by the age of 15 years 2 months," and, "fiercely individualistic" and "astonishingly precocious," only hesitated between research and teaching (newspapers, June 1964).

This is, no doubt, an extreme case, but it is surely inevitable that an institution equipped with such means of transmission should transmit something, if not necessarily what it wants to transmit and believes it transmits. In reality, contrary to appearances, the university always preaches to the converted. Given that its ultimate function is to ensure the acceptance of cultural values, it does not really need to constrain and sanction, because its clientele is defined by the more or less avowed aspiration to enter the intellectual class. But, since entry into the intelligentsia is a rational and reasonable aim for only a limited proportion of students, what can be the function of the fictitious, gamelike experience of intellectuality which all students have to pass through for several years, including those who will not become intellectuals?

The collective bad faith, whereby some students manage to avoid recognizing the true nature of their present work by avoiding recognition of the future for which it prepares them, is the first form of the "ruse of reason" in the logic of the university system. The symbolic execution of the intellectual calling, the performance—in the "let's pretend" mode—of the tasks of the accomplished intellectual, are, in one respect and for certain categories of students, one of the conditions of adherence to the values which dominate the intellectual world. Like the *normalien*[7] of the *belle époque*, the literature or philosophy student can still today live his undergraduate days as an initiatory retreat preparing him for an exclusively intellectual life, and perhaps it is (or used to be) necessary that it should be so. Instead of being seen merely as a means to an end, this apprenticeship is an end in itself. By autonomizing the present of studenthood, through a twofold negation of the *terminus a quo* and the *terminus ad quem*, the student can give himself the illusion of living the intellectual vocation to the full. This being so, apprenticeship in the games and tricks to be played with social determinisms must be seen as a valid occupational training, since it ensures the acquisition of the techniques by which the intellectual will be able to achieve real or fictitious experience of *freischwebende Intelligenz*.

This illusion is surely fostered by the very unreality of university practice. Even the specific sanctions and obligations seem to be dulled and blunted. A tacit complicity between students and teachers ensures that university discipline is neither imposed nor undergone as something imperious and ruthless; even if failure is experienced in dramatic terms, it never takes on the gravity of being fired from a job. By virtue of the character of the most serious sanction it contains, the examination, the university system is doubtless more akin to play than to work. But, on the one hand, the student, haunted by the anxious need to be something or somebody, is inclined toward a permanent self-questioning and, on the other hand, the teachers, imbued with the essentialist spirit which pervades an institution charged with establishing unquestioned hierarchies, feel entitled to judge the student's whole being, all the more so because they perceive the student's production, whether an exposé or a dissertation, as an exercise, a fictitious "performance," whose sole purpose is to manifest virtual and final, that is, essential, capacities. The student is thus impelled to seek in the value that the judgment of the school system sets on his "works," the one unquestionable sign of election. Teachers and students may perceive the unreality of scholastic tests and sanctions, and occasionally joke about them, without ceasing to invest them with the dramatic values of personal salvation.[8] The dissertation is unanimously felt to be a pretext for judging men, or, at least, the academic man, who exists in every man in modern societies and whom academics are not alone in regarding as the whole man. In more ways than one, the academic world calls to mind the world of a game, the field of validity of rules which are valid only insofar as one agrees to play the game, a circumscribed space and time set apart from the real world where economic and social factors make themselves felt; this is because, more than any other game, it proposes or imposes on those who play it the temptation to get caught up in the game by persuading them that their whole being is at stake in it.

And perhaps the challenging of the university and of university culture also conforms to the university model par excellence, the model of complicit, fictitious contestation, of the *disputatio de quolibet* and the *dissertatio de omni re scibili*, the supremely formal exercises through which the university teaches, under constraint, the exercise of intellectual freedom. Revolt against the school system and escape into heterodox enthusiasms achieve, by indirect routes, the ultimate ends pursued by the university. The most routine teacher, who, contrary to his intentions, provokes his students to espouse an "anti-culture" that they see as more vital and authentic, is still, despite himself, fulfilling his objective function—persuading the neophytes to worship culture and not the university, whose role is merely to organize the cult of culture. In short, by the supreme ruse of academic reason, constraint throws the most recalcitrant into adherence to values which fictitiously deny what the constraint serves. The seemingly most bohemian behavior is often only obedience to traditional models outside the field in which these models are traditionally applied, and the terrorists of culture are just star pupils playing hooky. Perhaps there would be less of a craze for the western if it were not seen as the Far West of culture. The film-club organizer hears the exposés or discussions which the literature or philosophy teacher strives, often in vain, to elicit. Thus, revolt against the external constraint of the rule is one of the ways in which the values the rule imposes are internalized; as in the Freudian myth, murdering the father inaugurates the reign of the introjected father.

It should come as no surprise that Parisian Arts faculty students present an *ideal-typical*, that is, at once complete and caricatural, image of the student as an intellectual novice, required to win his spurs as an autonomous intellectual by practicing the game whereby the art of disappointing expectations is the privileged mode of exercising intellectual freedom.

It is in Paris that there is the most marked refusal to allow the influence of family background on political opinions to show through. Whereas the University of Paris contains the highest proportion of students of bourgeois origin, the proportion of students who classify themselves as being on the left is higher here than in the provinces, where left-wing political opinions are very closely linked to membership of the underprivileged classes. It is also in Paris that there is the highest proportion of students who, while saying they are on the left, refuse to acknowledge affinities with a left-wing political party; and of those who feel the need to forge original labels to define themselves politically, such as "regenerated Trotskyism," "constructive anarchism," or "revolutionary neo-Communism," two thirds are Parisian. More generally, if, in their aesthetic choices, which often incline toward the avant-garde, or in their political choices, which are often extremist, Parisian students are, and seek to be, in declared opposition; if in their commitments they consciously choose to swim against the current, obedient to the conformism of anti-conformism, this is because the values of dilettantism and detachment which bourgeois students bring into the student world and which, especially in Paris, predominate in the student world as a whole, are closely related to the values which compose the intellectual ideal of free-floating intelligence.

This is why they, more than all others, are inclined to confound the symbolic breaks of adolescence with intellectual self-realization. Thus, a number of female students, many of whose choices continue to be governed by the most traditional intellectual models, realize their image of the liberated intellectual by breaking free from sexual norms. The high symbolic profitability of such liberations may be seen from the formal reversals which they make possible: "The valorization of virginity . . . gives way to a new 'mystique': the mystique of losing it at all costs."[9] And the charm of certain political commitments often lies partly in the fact that they offer the easiest and also the most scandalous way of symbolically consummating the break with one's family background. The typically intellectual game of distancing oneself from all limitations, whether social origin or occupational future, and the studies which prepare for it, calls forth and maintains the game of difference for difference's sake. The differences that derive from social origin are passed over in silence, while those that are deliberately expressed in opinions and tastes are manifest and manifested. There are few societies where sects clash, form, and dissolve so rapidly and through such complex processes; few groups where the play of polemics mobilizes such energies and arouses such passion. Thus, the minority faction in a group can oppose the majority in that group without joining the majority position in a larger group in which those with whom they disagree are themselves in the minority.[10]

Although most students only participate in these debates from a great distance and often have difficulty in deciding where they stand, the political ideas or aesthetic values over which and through which they oppose each other in endless argument all obey the same logic. The urge to distinguish oneself can operate equally well, and simultaneously, in the political field, the philosophical field, or in the aesthetic field. One Trotskyism opposes another, just as much as, in other ways, it opposes Maoism; the admirers of early Antonioni are opposed to fans of his second period, and both of these sects condemn Bergman, but on different grounds. In reality, the pursuit of difference presupposes a consensus on the limits within which the play of differences can operate and on the need to play the game within these limits. But, given the difficulty of finding real differences without going beyond the limits of the consensus, the oppositions are always liable to be fictitious or formal ones, and there is a risk of never discussing what is essential because one needs to agree on the essential in order to be able to argue.

The alliance of consensus and dissent within the limits of the consensus is most manifest in Paris. The proliferation of microgroups (*groupuscules*) and the conflicts between rival doctrines must not mask the fact that 79 percent of Paris Arts students say they are on the left, compared to 56 percent in the provinces, and that only 20 percent say they would never take part in student union activity, compared to 35 percent in the provinces. The body of required opinions remains roughly the same, even if it is given different overtones by different schools of thought. For example, while "commitments" are expressed in very different behaviors and vocabularies, the rule of the game is never to question the necessity of making a "commitment," or more precisely, a "concrete commitment." Similarly, students are capable of seeing the playlike character of their arguments without completely ceasing to take them seriously: "Are political discussions useful? They take up a lot of time but they're part of the daily routine" (senior executive's son, Paris). "There's a whole scene made up of meetings, and arguments in cafés, which may—well, they're not completely pointless. Anyway, they may be on political or social questions. Okay, they don't generally lead anywhere, but they do take up a certain amount of time" (shopkeeper's son, Paris). "Every day in the café: it might be seen as a pastime, anyway it's a moment of relaxation, a way of considering things that aren't directly discussed in school" (senior executive's son, Paris). "On Sunday evenings in my room, friends drop by and we talk politics; I suppose you could call it a pastime" (senior executive's son, Paris).

Pressure directly exerted by this milieu does not explain either the strength of the consensus or the taste for formal oppositions within the limits of the consensus, for, as we have seen, in Paris, the student milieu is less integrated than anywhere else. Ideological games are doubtless only one aspect of a whole attitude toward studenthood and intellectual life which a privileged situation normally authorizes. Since no clear distinction is generally made between conditions of existence and conditions of work, it is not usually realized that the conditions of existence of Paris students are considerably better than those of provincial students. Paris has the highest proportion of students from the wealthiest classes, the highest proportion of students living with their parents or receiving financial support from them, and the lowest proportion of students deriving their income from paid employment. Given that the cultural advantages regularly associated with bourgeois origin are reinforced by residence in Paris, it is not surprising that bourgeois Paris students, compounding all the privileges, should be capable of manifesting, more than all other students, the casualness and detachment vis-à-vis their studies which are the acknowledged sign of intellectual mastery, and should be more inclined than others to the political audacities which bring them the satisfactions of an adherence to the intellectual consensus that is apparently all the more meritorious for being deliberate.

But the most important differences, at least as far as deep-seated attitudes are concerned, stem perhaps from the nature of the relationships which Parisians and provincials have to the university institution, the faculty staff, and the intellectual milieu. Paris students, by virtue of their closeness to the center of intellectual values, feel its attraction more strongly. The proximity of the literary and philosophical coteries, knowledge of the nuances which separate them and which are only perceptible to those initiated personally or at one remove, or, more precisely, to those who belong by birth to the restricted or extended family of intellectuals—in short, the whole capital of information which is only acquired by frequenting seminars, lectures, debates, or assemblies, by reading fashionable journals or taking part in *groupuscules,* where there is always some well-informed intermediary eager to pass on the latest news, give a spice of gossip to the great theoretical debates and authorize a familiarity, at once reverent and irreverent, that is perfectly analogous to the familiarity with which the common people of Rome indulge in disrespectful chatter about the respectable secrets of the Curia.

Moreover, there is greater dependence on university tutelage in the provinces than in Paris. For the Parisian student, the multiplicity of professors supplies the means of relativizing the prestige (if not the authority) of each professor and, more radically, the diversity of the intellectual world supplies the means of relativizing professorial prestige. The provincial student is condemned to the university and to the university professor who reigns unchallenged in his discipline. More tied to academic constraints even in his least academic interests, he is less inclined to live his student days as an intellectual adventure.

Thus, everything predisposes Paris literary students to enter the games of literary Paris. Their training has equipped them with an arsenal of rhetoric and given them the taste for ideas; and they are made to feel even more justified in entering the ideological debates of the day by the fact that they are objectively invited to do so by their situation as a public whose approval is competed for. But when they do intervene, as they are doing now, à propos of the crisis in education, they tend to bring into the debate their grand ambitions and their minor dramas, expanding to a universal scale an experience which they are prone to live through and conceive in universal terms because they live it and think it in an academic universe whose mission is to think universally. Thus, because in literature, philosophy, or the social sciences, the frontier between sententious chatter and scientific discussion is more blurred than elsewhere, and knowledge acquired by hearsay is less likely to be seen for what it is, students in these subjects can make what is only a beginner's illusion the basis for a universal reflection on education. It may also be that ideological games are one way of overcoming an anxious and unhappy experience of the student situation. The pursuit of originality at all costs doubtless has a particularly vital function for the Parisian student, who finds himself in extremely difficult working conditions and at all times feels the unease aroused by threatening contact with a host of unknown rivals. The most readily avowed experiences, such as those of being overwhelmed or isolated, may perhaps express, in a "displaced" form, the student's fundamental anxiety. Constantly forced to ask himself "What am I worth?", knowing no other sign of election than academic success, he feels failure and anonymity as assaults on his very being. Like the efforts or tricks to catch the professor's attention (to "get into his good books") or their opposite, sneers and denigration, ideological debates are one of the ways of escaping this virtual experience of abandonment.

The myth of self-education, an aristocratic utopia characteristic of small groups of the elect who set out to decide for themselves the goals of their own activity, has had considerable success recently, perhaps because this ideology fulfilled the deepest and least acknowledged wishes of bourgeois Parisian students by setting up a permanent feast. In festivity, a group can affirm its integration by fictitiously intensifying its symbolic exchanges; it can savor more fully the gratifications accruing from integration, reveling in the image of itself as an integrated group, in a game of integration which has no other aim than to reinforce integration.[11]

It is difficult to recognize what really divides and unites students, difficult to distinguish what is play and what is genuine in their commitments, because the ideologies and images arising from the traditional relation to culture condemn university teachers' and students' practice to take hold of reality only indirectly and symbolically, that is, through the veil of rhetorical illusion. To construct the model of the relationship between the ideologies and the objective significance of the behavior, it is necessary to consider the extreme case, in which the traditional relation to culture that is encouraged and perpetuated by the literary disciplines is combined with the intense contact with the intellectual world that is favored by living in Paris and with the risk-free freedom that a well-to-do social origin makes possible. A student who combines these traits, that is, in the limiting case, the Parisian Arts student whose father is an intellectual, regarded as the *ideal type* of the traditional student, constructs a representation of his situation which can be seen as the inverted image of his true situation. By means of a systematic reversal, the sociology of ideologies reveals the identity that the declared differences conceal and the differences hidden behind the declared identity.[12]

If it is the case that the major determinant of attitudes is social origin, and if it is also the case that students from the bourgeoisie are still in the majority and that the values they owe to their milieu continue to influence them and, through them, students from other classes, then it is legitimate to consider that the student milieu owes a number of its characteristics to the group which continues to predominate in number and status. New recruits to the intelligentsia are drawn primarily from among students of bourgeois origin because the play of free intelligence presupposes that studenthood be approached as a game excluding all sanctions other than those defined by the rules of the game, rather than as an apprenticeship subject to the test of occupational success. It follows that with an increase in the proportion of working-class students, bringing in new values and a necessarily more realistic experience of the student situation, there will be a move away from the *ideal-typical* description in which the traits of the dominant group are applied to students as a whole; less rapidly, however, because even when students of bourgeois origin cease to be numerically preponderant, the norms and values they have bequeathed to the student milieu will not cease to be regarded as inseparable from that milieu, even by social categories making their first entry into higher education.

The student situation does not condemn all categories of students to an unreal, playlike experience in any undifferentiated, uniform way. Students are undeniably serious in their approach to the questions they are asking themselves about their present and future roles. This has especially been the case in the last few

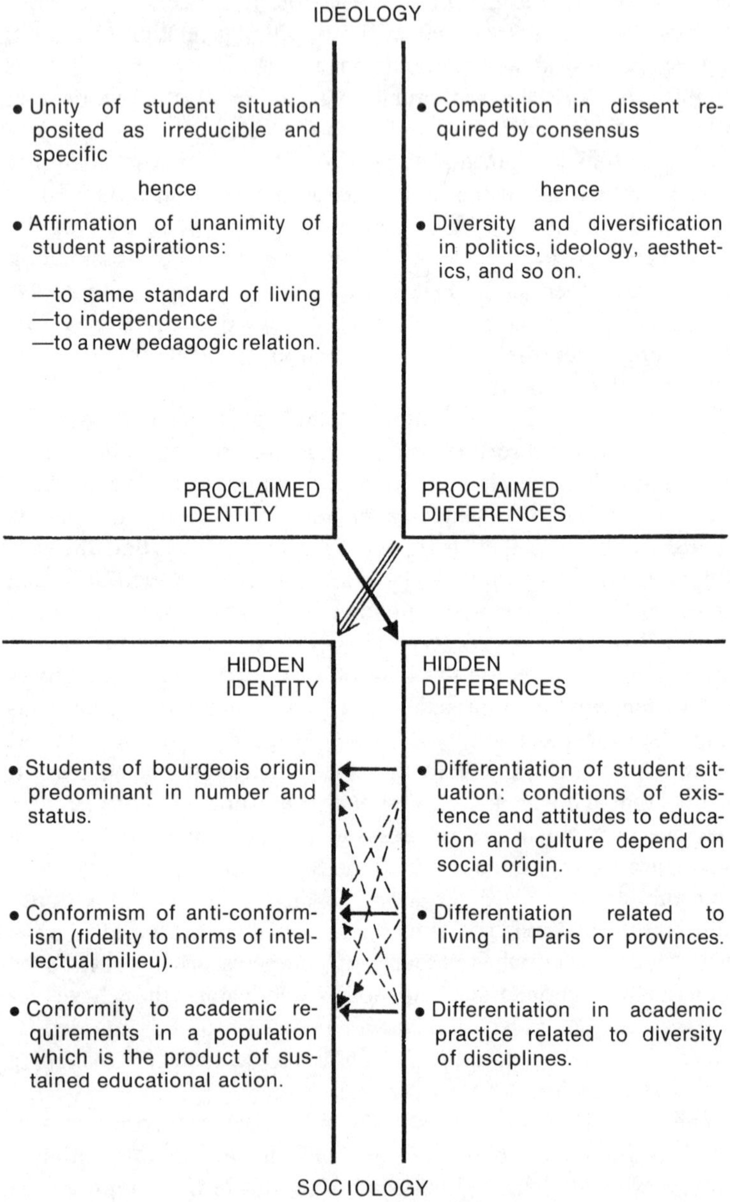

IDEOLOGY

- Unity of student situation posited as irreducible and specific

  hence

- Affirmation of unanimity of student aspirations:

  —to same standard of living
  —to independence
  —to a new pedagogic relation.

- Competition in dissent required by consensus

  hence

- Diversity and diversification in politics, ideology, aesthetics, and so on.

PROCLAIMED
IDENTITY

PROCLAIMED
DIFFERENCES

HIDDEN
IDENTITY

HIDDEN
DIFFERENCES

- Students of bourgeois origin predominant in number and status.

- Conformism of anti-conformism (fidelity to norms of intellectual milieu).

- Conformity to academic requirements in a population which is the product of sustained educational action.

- Differentiation of student situation: conditions of existence and attitudes to education and culture depend on social origin.

- Differentiation related to living in Paris or provinces.

- Differentiation in academic practice related to diversity of disciplines.

SOCIOLOGY

Fig. 5

years, and it is significant that they explicitly address themselves to the question of their own seriousness. But the unreality of the student situation does not vanish just because students decide they want to be serious. Rather, it may be an intensified sense of the unreality of academic experience that engenders not only serious questions about the seriousness of studenthood but also unreal questions about real problems.

We must distinguish between the unreality conferred on the student's experience by the fact that his situation is not a profession, and the anti-realism to which privileged conditions of existence are conducive. The anti-realist tendency does not depend solely on the degree of unreality in the situation. Thus, the futile and frivolous experience that a bourgeois student of the old tradition (a lawyer's son certain to become a lawyer) could have of his studenthood drew very little on the intrinsic unreality of the student situation; by contrast, present-day Arts students may know nothing of the bohemian revelry of the students of the past and yet feel the unreality of the future which their most visible behavior takes as its reference and which they call for with their deepest wishes. If they are of petit-bourgeois or working-class origin, they may even feel the unreality of a teaching little changed in its methods or sometimes even in its content, because it is ill-suited to the expectations and interests their background has given them or perhaps because they measure it against an occupational future with which they have a more realistic concern. Furthermore, indifference to realities is never so great that it prevents behaviors and attitudes from being, consciously or unconsciously, organized by reference to the objective likelihood of actually occupying the role for which the student is being prepared. Thus, the degree of commitment to the intellectal game and to the values it implies is never independent of social origin. The term *seriousness*, therefore, covers two distinct ways of living studenthood. One of them is primarily characteristics of students of bourgeois origin who make higher education an experience into which enter no problems more serious than those they put there. The other expresses the anxiety about the future characteristic of students who have come from the social strata that are furthest from academic culture and who are condemned to experience that culture as unreal. It follows that denunciations of unreality are not all equally serious and that the most serious experience of unreality is not necessarily conducive to realism.

3·Sorcerers' Apprentices

T HE NECESSITY FOR EDUCATION IS PRESENT IN
children as their own feeling of dissatisfaction with themselves
as they are. . . . The play theory of education assumes that what
is childish is itself already something of inherent worth and
presents it as such to the children; in their eyes it lowers serious
pursuits, and education itself, to a form of childishness for which
the children themselves have scant respect. The advocates of
this method represent the child, in the immaturity in which he
feels himself to be, as really mature and they struggle to make
him satisfied with himself as he is. But they corrupt and distort
his genuine and proper need for something better, and create
in him a blind indifference to the substantial ties of the
intellectual world, a contempt of his elders because they have
thus posed before him, a child, in a contemptible and childish
fashion, and finally a vanity and conceit which feeds on the notion
of its own superiority.

Hegel, *Philosophy of Right.*

To understand how and why the student's situation contains the
objective possibility of an unreal or mystified relation to his studies
and to the future for which they prepare him, it is necessary to
construct, at least for heuristic purposes, the *ideal type* of perfectly rational student conduct. This would be conduct which
exclusively applied means that are regarded as adequate with a
view to achieving univocally posited ends. Even if this fictitious
construct is as far from reality as it could possibly be, it is in no
way an ideal, since it is obtained by logical development of the
reality implied in the fact of being a student or being in the student situation. Not only is the significance of actual conducts
better understood when they are contrasted with the ideal-typi-
cally rational conduct which has the self-evidence of all rational
conduct; but further, by making completely explicit what is in-

volved in the rational performance of study, one is able to evaluate the distance between rational conduct and the actual conducts of the different categories of students. More precisely, it is possible to measure these conducts, not against an arbitrarily chosen norm, but against the constructed model of what student conduct would be if it perfectly corresponded to what it claims to be in some of its ideological expressions, that is, perfectly rational in terms of the ends which it posits by its very existence. If it turns out that the model of conduct constructed on the hypothesis of correspondence to rational ends objectively inscribed in the student situation takes on the air of a utopia when compared with students' actual conducts, and makes the millenarian ideologies of certain student groups appear utopian, that will be because it has fulfilled its function as a touchstone of the rationality and realism of conducts and ideologies.

The fact has to be faced: a student's creativity can only ever be a self-creation. Only rhetorical exuberance can lead one to forget what makes the very definition of the student's role: to study is not to create something but to create oneself; it is not to create a culture, still less a new culture, but to create one's capacity to be, at best, a creator of culture, or, in most cases, an informed user or transmitter of a culture created by others, that is, a teacher or specialist. More generally, to study is not to produce, but to produce a capacity to produce.

This does not mean that the student is cast into a passive role, as if there were no alternative between ingurgitation and creation. The romantic image of intellectual work and an impatience of self-imposed disciplines lead some people to reject as an insult to the student intelligence the specific activity of the *apprentice intellectual,* namely, the learning of intellectual activity by training and exercise. But the organizing of fictitious "practice" is the school's way of developing mastery of future practices.

In other words, the student has and can have no other task than to work toward his own disappearance qua student.[1] This would presuppose that he acknowledge himself as a student and as a temporary student: to work toward his own disappearance qua student would then be to work toward the disappearance of the teacher qua teacher by appropriating that of which he is a teacher, being aided in this by the teacher, who would set himself the task of working toward his own disappearance qua teacher. This is sufficient to show that the mystification par excellence consists in magically denying oneself qua student by denying the teacher qua teacher through the utopia of participation in the creation of culture, that is, by believing that one is abolishing oneself qua student when one is merely refusing to be a student without undertaking the effort of negation.

The models of professorial conduct and student conduct constructed on the hypothesis of rational ends and means are, clearly, equally remote from present-day reality. Thus, teachers and students may concur in denouncing student passivity without thereby ceasing to take advantage of the benefits of such passivity. It is all too obvious that, especially in Paris, the student is condemned always to be the passive term in the pedagogic relationship. If the student sees himself as an acted-upon subject devoid of initiative and, like a statue of Condillac, reduced to pure receptivity, this is because, in reality, his whole activity is that of recording. He accumulates knowledge, materially and mentally, is dispensed from creating, especially from practicing creation, and is purely the receptacle of professorial knowledge. But to impute this state of affairs solely to the conservatism of authoritarian professors dispenses one from analyzing the deep satisfactions which it gives to students. Such an analysis would make it easier to understand the satisfactions which it also gives to the professors. A teacher never asks for as much passivity as the students grant him, and a professorial invitation to participate actively is no more capable of overcoming the ingrained passivity of students formed by the system and subject to its logic than the student Spartacism which rejects professorial oppression in the name of the myth of student creativity, as if the only alternative to passivity were creation.

Just as everyone agrees, without drawing the same conclusions, that the definition of a student is someone who studies, so it will readily be accepted that to be a student is to prepare oneself by study for an occupational future. But it is not superfluous to draw out all the implications of this formula. It implies, first of all, that the action of studying is a means to an end which is external to it; it also implies that present action takes on its full meaning only in terms of a future which the present prepares for by preparing its own negation. It follows that a situation which is defined as provisional and transitional can only derive its seriousness from the occupational situation for which it prepares, or, in other words, that here the present has reality only vicariously and proleptically. Therefore, if this logic is followed through, the most rational way of doing the job of being a student would be to organize all one's present action with a view to the demands of one's occupational future and to apply all the rational means to attain this explicitly posited end as quickly and as completely as possible.[2]

The reality is quite different. Everything takes place as if, with the self-interested complicity of their teachers, students unconsciously strove to conceal from themselves the true nature of their work, by separating their present from their future, the means from the ends they are supposed to serve. If what students do, that is, what they are made to do, often appears to them as a "make-believe" or an "acting as if," this is because work is here not accompanied, as it is elsewhere, by the serious, tangible gratifications that directly follow occupational tasks. A future linked to the present by too many mediations is always liable to be experienced as fictitious, and fictitiously. The autonomization of an essentially provisional, transitional state enables the student to forget himself qua student, by forgetting his future. To this end, university tradition offers him two major models, apparently contradictory but equally approved, the "exam-hound" (*"bête à concours"*) and the "dilettante."[3] The former, fascinated by scholastic success, puts out of his mind everything beyond the examination, not least the qualification which the examination is supposed to guarantee. The student "polarized" by the narrow horizon of scholastic deadlines contrasts, in appearance, with the "dilettante" who knows only the infinitely retreating horizons of intellectual adventure. The illusion of apprenticeship as an end in itself realizes the aspiration toward the status of an intellectual, an eternal apprentice, but only in a magical mode, because it has to deny the ends which apprenticeship really serves, namely, entry to a profession, even an intellectual one. In either case, there is the same endeavor to give the present a fictitious immobility, by making it eternal or autonomous, when objectively it calls for its own abolition.

These two ways of living the student life without outliving it can happily coexist among students and sometimes even in the same student, because they are produced and encouraged by the whole university system and because they supply the professors—the students' opponents and accomplices—with reasons and means to lead the academic life that suits them. If ever the student formed a rational and realistic image of his position, the professor would find himself confronted with demands which relegate him to the role of a teaching auxiliary. The professor's occupational task would then become merely an aspect of an occupational project of which he is no longer the master and whose full significance lies beyond him. Just as certain students magically deny the teacher qua teacher, so, too, a good many teachers who deploy every charismatic trick to deny the possibility of their own negation as masters, would absolutely reject this instrumental role.

A mystified experience of the student situation is the basis for an enchanted experience of the professorial function. Instead of the technically contrived matching of an instructor and a trainee, there can be an elective encounter between two members of the elect. Because it enables the teachers to see themselves as masters communicating a total culture by personal gift, this interplay of reciprocal and complementary indulgence obeys the logic of a system which, like the French system in its present form, seems to serve traditional rather than rational ends and to work objectively to fashion men of culture rather than men with a trade. The professorial lecture itself is another exchange, since the virtuoso's prowess is implicitly addressed to persons worthy of receiving and appreciating it. University exchange is a gift exchange in which each partner grants the other what he expects in return, the recognition of his own gift.[4]

However, students do not all have an equally false relation to their present position, because the future is not equally unreal, indeterminate, or disenchanting for all of them. Distance from the rational project is a function of the objective likelihood of the future most strongly hoped for; and this likelihood varies considerably, depending on the nature of the desired occupational future and on the present situation of each category of students. An Arts student is always likely to have a more indeterminate image of his eventual occupation than a medical student or a pupil of the Ecole Nationale d'Administration. Even within the Arts faculties, the disciplines with uncertain post-graduation employment prospects, such as sociology, seem to attract those students whose vocation is most uncertain and also to favor vocational uncertainty. When the occupational future is clearly and firmly linked to the present, that is, to study, scholastic exercises are immediately subordinated to the occupational tasks which give them a meaning and a *raison d'être*; by contrast, the Arts student, haunted by the uncertainty and vagueness of his future, is forced to identify scholastic exercises with intellectual adventure in order to preserve the meaningfulness of his undertaking. The philosophy student does not and cannot see himself as a future philosophy teacher, because he needs to forget that destination in order to reach it. Here, mystified experience is one of the conditions for adherence to the values involved in one's very practice. The most illogical images of one's work are not always totally without logic in the literary disciplines, where the idea of rationalizing the means is always liable to be seen as incompatible with the nature of the ends, these being more traditional than rational, or, at the very least, as threatening to deprive both the studies and the intellectual career for which they prepare of what makes all their charm, often in the absence of any other gratification.

Because, for female students, entry into an occupation is particularly improbable, they are also obliged to endeavor to conceal from themselves a future which might well take away all meaning from their present or give it a flavor quite opposite to what they want to find in it. But their objective future imposes itself so clearly that, in their case, mystification can never completely succeed, so that the key to a good deal of their behavior can only be found in the objective truth of their situation. The difference between the sexes appears most clearly in the conducts or opinions which involve self-image or anticipation of the future. Although female students' living and working conditions are becoming more and more like those of male students, and although they are more inclined than other women to refuse the traditional feminine place in society, it should not be concluded that all female students have traveled equally far, in all areas, from the traditional models. The most obvious models, too manifestly associated with a role that is repudiated, are most likely to provoke resistance or revolt, whereas no less traditional models that are less clearly perceived can continue to exert an influence, albeit an unconscious one, because they continue to determine the objective, collective future.

> Female students, especially those drawn from the bourgeoisie, have a confused grasp of the future: "I really love being a student, it's the happiest time of your life, the time when you can do what you enjoy . . . You're free to do anything, it's the time to enrich your personality" (student,

Paris, age 20, publisher's daughter). "It's just great being a
student, you're so free" (student, Paris, 20, doctor's
daughter). "A student is moving toward something, it's a
time of expectation, the important thing is to feel you are being
productive" (student, 20, Paris, ambassador's daughter).
"It's the time when you decide where you're heading; you can
be a student all your life, it's a kind of work like any other.
You're responsible for what you do and you're trying to
progress intellectually" (student, Paris, 21, university teacher's
daughter). "Students don't feel happy about what they're
learning . . . I don't feel I'm being useful at present . . . Am
I, as a Frenchwoman, going to be able to make use of what
I've learned, in society as it now is? As far as my career's
concerned, I'll get by, but in a larger context, I'm not sure"
(student Paris, 21, senior executive's daughter). Reference to
the category's objective future seems to start very early,
since one finds it expressed in the *lycée*, by girls of 14 or 15,
not only in their choice of supposedly "feminine" occupations
—teacher, educational psychologist, interior decorator—but
also in their concern, often explicitly stated, to save themselves
for domestic tasks by working only part-time.

Young men and women from the same social category differ
not so much in the objective likelihood of their entering university
as in the objective likelihood of their studying this or that subject, largely because the young women's parents and the young
women themselves continue to accept an image of the specifically
feminine "qualities" or "gifts" that is still dominated by the traditional model of the sexual division of labor.[5] Similarly, it can
be assumed that the differences between male and female students
regarding their conditions of existence (type of accommodation,
for example) to some extent reflect the image which parents, and
female students themselves, have of the degree of freedom appropriate to young men and to young women. More generally, the
differences between the sexes are most marked in the behaviors or
attitudes linked to the least conscious aspects of self-image. More
female students intend to go into teaching than men, a preference
which expresses a concern, stronger in the provinces than in
Paris, not to repudiate the traditional tasks of womanhood.[6]
Women have a more modest opinion of their academic worth and
a more humble attitude toward the techniques of intellectual work
than do men of equal scholastic ability. Another indication of

their greater difficulty in experiencing studenthood as an intellectual vocation may be seen in the fact that they read fewer philosophical and sociological works than male students, whereas they devote much the same amount of time per week to their scholastic work.[7] It is as if, feeling more acutely the unreality of the least scholastic cultural activities, the female student endeavored to use scholastic zeal and docility as a way of avoiding the question of the future for which her studies are preparing her. The differences one finds in political and student-union involvement can be explained in terms of the same logic. In the student world, politics remains, at least implicitly, a male preserve: student-union leaders frequently attribute students' apathy toward their unions to the high proportion of female students and are reluctant to entrust to women those tasks reputed to be the most serious. Less politicized, less left-inclined than the men, the women have a smaller share of union responsibilities; they read fewer newspapers, and those they do read are less political.[8]

The specificity of the women's relation to the dominant values of the student milieu and the difficulties they encounter when trying to reconstruct a unified image of their role are most strikingly highlighted in the style of their remarks about "commitment." For the most part sharing the specific ideological consensus of the student milieu, two-thirds of them declare themselves to be "committed," and those who are not apologize for it. But everything they say reveals their fidelity to a traditional definition of the tasks of woman. Only exceptionally does one hear a utilitarian or rational justification for "serving others," but there is an abundance of metaphors exalting the ideal of sacrifice, a vestige of the traditional ethic. The vocabulary of *contact* and *relationship* alternates with that of *enrichment* and *blossoming of the personality* or with the moral vocabulary of *presence as a duty*: "Having enriching human contact." "Meeting people." "Cooperation with other people." "An opportunity for lots of contact and dialogue." "Enables me to devote myself to others." "Discovering other people." "Personal development, opening up to other people." "An endeavor to be more responsive to other people." "Helping others; personal enrichment." "Feeling in sympathy with those around me, developing my personality." "Unfolding my personality, contact." "Fulfillment and encounters." "Helps me relate to other people." "Better understanding of others and development of myself." "Enriching myself and others." "Something to discover and something to give." "Personal enrichment." "A way of devoting myself." "Personal fulfillment by making a sacrifice." "Self-affirmation, self-realization, putting my ideas into practice, giving substance to an abstract ideal." "Spiritual enrichment." "A point of stability in my life." "A lever, the fulcrum of my work." "Something serious and indispensable." "One of the essential ways of taking part in human transcendence." "A concrete means of assuming one's responsibilities." "My place is in the service of others." "Responsibility for others." "The goal to which all that is Human tends." "Justice. Peace. Virtue. Freedom. Love."

In short, because their present is dominated by the image of a future which belies or questions it, female students cannot unconditionally espouse the values of the intelligentsia and are less successful than men in concealing from themselves the unreality of their present by acting as if their future were unreal. And if scholastic docility offers itself to them as the least bad way of managing to do so, this is perhaps because it constitutes a felicitous reinterpretation of the traditional model of female dependence which, in this case, perfectly matches the expectations of a higher education system that has remained traditional (and male-oriented) in its spirit (and its teaching staff).

As for the male students, their distance from rational conduct and their attitude toward the seductions of the intellectual vocation vary mainly as a function of their social origin. A number of features suggest that, in terms of their relation to the future, females are to males as lower-class students are to upper-class students. The objectively lesser likelihood that they will have an occupation and especially an intellectual one (a likelihood which always counts in behavior even when refused in ideology) prohibits them from launching into the intellectual game with all the ardor that comes only from the risk-free forgetting of a guaranteed future. Lower-class students, forced to entertain more realistic occupational projects, can never completely abandon themselves to dilettantism or fall for the occasional glamor of studies which remain, for them, essentially an opportunity to be seized, of rising in the social hierarchy. Bowing to necessity, they more often know and acknowledge the occupation for which they are preparing and the fact that they are preparing for an occupation. The relation students have to their futures, that is, to their studies, varies as a direct function of the objective chances which individuals of their class have of entering higher education, so that upper-class students can be satisfied with vague projects because they have never really had to choose to do what they are doing—studenthood being an everyday occurrence in their milieu and even in their own families—whereas lower-class students cannot fail to wonder what they are doing because they are less likely to forget that they might not have been able to do it.

So we have seen that studenthood can only derive its seriousness from the occupational future for which it prepares, or, more precisely, from the student's taking that preparation seriously. We have seen too that, for different reasons and through varied means, students, and especially the most privileged students, generally conceal from themselves the objective truth of their situation. It is therefore understandable that they should rarely be inclined to organize their practice rationally by reference to the occupational tasks they will have to perform and that, often maintaining a mystified relation to their work, they attach little interest and value to acquiring the techniques, or even the knacks, that would enable them to organize their learning in a methodical way with a view to a rational end, posited explicitly and unambiguously. For example, teachers and aspiring teachers generally concur in contempt for pedagogy, in other words for one of the areas of knowledge most specifically linked to what they do or will have to do. Similarly, every attempt to reintroduce "scholastic" discipline into higher education is immediately perceived by students and teachers as offensive to the dignity of the former and incompatible with the mastery of the latter.

Here, too, students and teachers collaborate in the exchange of prestigious images: a professor who undertook to teach the material techniques of intellectual work—how to compile a card-index system or draw up a bibliography, for example—would abdicate his authority as a "master" and, in the eyes of the students whose self-image he had violated, would appear as a vulgar schoolmaster who had somehow stumbled into higher education. Inside every student is a Péguy, the man who called Mauss "Mr. Filing-card Boxes." As for intellectual techniques, such as the ability to define the concepts used or the elementary principle of rhetoric and logic, students regard them, when, that is, they know of their existence, as unacceptable constraints or unseemly gadgets, sullying the romantic image of intellectual work as free, inspired creation. In the absence of any rational relation to the probable future, the present becomes a dreamworld from which the very notion of efficient techniques and technical efficiency is excluded.

So it is no accident that the occupational "techniques" most often observed in the student world almost always partake of magic. It is true that, by encouraging passivity and dependence, the logic of the system tends to place the student in a situation which cannot be entirely mastered by rational means. For example, by devaluing the role of guidelines for success and sometimes ingeniously disguising the material and intellectual techniques which are the basis (sometimes the sole basis) of their charisma, by omitting or avoiding any clear statement of the criteria of their judgments, the professors of wizardry can only reinforce their students' sense of impotence, arbitrariness, or predestined failure. On their side, because they find it more agreeable and less demanding to place their faith in charisma than laboriously to master techniques, students are condemned to entertain an image of academic success on which, if the "gift" is lacking, only magic can have any effect.

Ethnological inquiry shows that students respond to the fear of examinations with a whole range of nostrums, simultaneously magical and technical, partly inherited from the tradition, partly reinvented by each individual, to overcome, or, rather, exorcise, the same dangers. In this context, apparently rational procedures become blind observances conforming to the logic of magical formalism: feverish revision on the night before an examination is often nothing more than a set of propitiatory rites; taking notes that will never be read again is a technique for spiritual consolation rather than rational accumulation. "After an hour's scribbling, you're sick of it. You never look back over your lecture notes. Anyway, they're illegible" (Arts student, 22, Paris, senior executive's daughter). Students hand down as infallible charms the art of placing one's script underneath that of an acknowledged ignoramus or choosing the right moment to appear before an oral examiner. A host of superstitions, the like of which is perhaps found only in the traditional peasant who depends on the whims of nature, or in the world of gambling, surrounds the perilous moments of university life: prognostication rites to forecast the questions or the marks, propitiatory or grateful ex-votos deposited in churches, amulets or fetishes brought into the examination room, such are the commonest means of forcing the hand of chance. "Holy Virgin, thank You for my examination," or "An hour from now I take my examination; Holy Mary, pray for me," such are the inscriptions to be seen in the cathedral in Poitiers, a university town, either engraved into the marble or written on other ex-votos. In addition to those who seek to master chance by means of an extraordinary ritual, are others who, by applying the principle of magical reiteration, remain faithful to conduct that has succeeded in the past or to objects which, having accompanied that success, have been imbued with its essence, such as the suit or tie worn at the last examination. If the art of "gambling" on the questions that may come up occupies such an important place in examination stories, this is because it constitutes the most striking demonstration of academic *mana*, success bearing witness to the magnitude of a gift that is sufficiently sure of itself to expect no advantage from work.

Maintaining a contradictory relation to his future, the student is able to combine an overt contempt for the means that would enable him to master it with a secret faith in the nostrums and formulas, more magical than technical, that enable him to exorcize its threats.

Thus, there is a vast distance between the rational model of student or professorial conduct and the actual conduct of students and professors. Students and professors are perhaps united in the secret desire to preserve the hidden advantages which the present system gives them, while at the same time enjoying the manifest advantages they would get from the opposite system which is, as such, incompatible with the present system. Just as teachers can deplore student passivity without seeing that it is the counterpart of the security they owe to an assymetric pedagogic relation, so some students can attribute the passivity in which they are kept solely to professorial authoritarianism, without seeing that it is the price to be paid for all the safety and freedom they derive from the anonymity of the lecture theater. Professors and students can even agree in vehemently denouncing the obstacles to a rationalization of education; failing to grasp the system as a whole, they cannot and do not want to see that the contradictory, but simultaneously or alternately obtainable, satisfactions it gives them are necessarily linked to the shortcomings they deplore.

And, indeed, it is neither agreeable nor easy to make a complete assessment of the costs of the present system. A system that would subordinate the choice of its pedagogic means to a single end, namely, the training of specialists (even if they are general specialists), can doubtless never be more than a utopia: a real educational system, charged with producing values by reference to values which are none other than those of the society for which it produces them, is always invested with multiple, incommensurate functions, so that it is not possible to emphasize one or another of them without bringing in the ultimate values that a society, or, rather, the groups of which it is composed, put into their representation of culture. However, it makes a difference whether primacy is really given to one goal rather than another, for example, to the perpetuation of an elite of cultivated individuals or to the diversified preparation of the greatest number for occupational tasks. The *ideal type* of "rational" education is an abstract fiction resulting from the methodological decision to accentuate, one-sidedly and by means of an unrealizable limiting case, the features of a system that would define and fully create the technical conditions for intellectual apprenticeship; it shows, by comparison, that the various goals that an educational system can serve are unequally distant from the goals that, explicitly or not, the different groups assign to education, and, therefore, corresponds unequally to their different interests.

It is particularly important here to distinguish between the functions an educational system performs and the means by which it performs them. The link which we find, in practice, between the most traditional values and the pedagogic tradition of mastery might easily make one forget that rational means could be employed in the service of ends diametrically opposed to those implied in the learning of strictly defined vocational tasks. The rationalization of the art of transmitting adherence to cultural values, for example, in the teaching of literature or aesthetic disciplines, is, after all, no more inconceivable than the rationalization of, religious life, in Max Weber's sense. In any event, if there can be debate about the goals of the sort of education most likely to serve the interests of the disadvantaged classes, the fact remains that in the present state of the French system and of the ends to which it is oriented, the rationalization of pedagogic methods and institutions is always immediately consistent with the interests of the most disadvantaged students.

Conclusion

REMEMBER, GENTLEMEN, JOHN CHRYSOS-
tom's exquisite story about the day he entered the rhetorician
Libanius' school in Antioch. Whenever a new pupil arrived at his
school, Libanius would question him about his past, his parents
and his country.

Renan, La Réforme intellectuelle et morale

Blindness to social inequalities both obliges and allows one to
explain all inequalities, particularly those in educational achievement, as natural inequalities, unequal giftedness.[1] Such an attitude
is part of the logic of a system which is based on the postulate
of the formal equality of all pupils, as a precondition of its operation, and cannot recognize any inequalities other than those arising from individual gifts. Whether in teaching or in selecting, the
teacher only acknowledges pupils equal in rights and duties. If, in
the course of the academic year, he decides to modify his teaching
for the sake of certain students, then he is addressing himself to
"the less gifted" and not to those most disadvantaged by their
social origin; and if on the day of the examination, he makes allowance for the social situation of this or that candidate, this is
not because he perceives him as a member of a disadvantaged
class, but because he grants him the exceptional interest which a
"social case" deserves. Verbal exorcism can be used to drive away
the very idea of a link between students' culture and their social
origin when this connection presents itself in the form of gross
lacunae. To say in a tone of resigned disapproval that "students
don't read anything nowadays" or that "the standard gets worse
every year" is to avoid considering why this is so and drawing the
appropriate pedagogic conclusions from it.

It is understandable that the crowning glory of this system
should be the national competitive examination, the *concours*,

which perfectly ensures the candidates' formal equality but which, through anonymity, precludes any allowance for real cultural inequalities. The champions of the *agrégation* can legitimately argue that, as opposed to a system of selection based on caste and birth, the *concours* gives everyone an equal opportunity. They forget that the formal equality provided by the *concours* merely transforms privilege into merit, since it allows the influence of social origin to operate, though through more secret channels.

But could things be different? Among other functions, the educational system is required to produce individuals who are selected and arranged in a hierarchy once and for all, for their whole lifetime. Within this logic, to seek to take account of social privileges or disadvantages and to undertake to arrange individuals in a hierarchy according to their real merit, that is, according to the obstacles overcome, would require, if the logic were followed through *ad absurdum*, either competition within categories (as in boxing) or, as in the estimation of merits in Kantian ethics, evaluation of the algebraic differences between each person's starting point, that is, his socially conditioned abilities, and his point of arrival, that is, his scholastically measured achievement—in short, classification in terms of handicap. Just as Kant attributes unequal merits to two intrinsically equivalent actions when they are performed by two "temperaments" unequally inclined to such actions, so here, substituting consideration of socially conditioned ability for that of natural inclination, one would have to examine not the level of achievement recorded at a given point but its relation to the point of departure, which may be more or less high or low—that is, not the point but the slope of the curve.[2] Within this logic, estimating the handicaps of individuals from the disadvantaged classes and evaluating the degrees of merit corresponding to the magnitude of the handicap overcome would—if this were possible—lead one to regard the producers of unequal performances as equal and the producers of equal performances as unequal. This would relativize the hierarchy established on the scholastic criterion and cancel out the benefit which the disadvantaged individuals, thereby *artificially* favored, would derive from this demagogic relativizing of the hierarchy. Such a hypothesis is not entirely utopian. The educational policy of the people's democracies may have tended systematically to favor the university entrance and examination success of the children of workers and peasants. But the equalizing endeavor remains a formal one so long as inequalities are not actually removed by pedagogic action. Thus, in Poland, after having risen until 1957, the proportion of students from rural and working-class backgrounds started to fall as soon as administrative pressure was relaxed.[3]

If the idea of making allowance for social handicaps is just as alien to those who have the task of selection as to those who are selected, this is perhaps because, in order to produce selected and selectable individuals, the educational system has to obtain, and therefore to produce, unquestioned adherence to a selection principle which the introduction of alternative principles would necessarily relativize. It requires those who enter the game to accept the rules of a competition in which only scholastic criteria count. And it seems to succeed in this, especially in France, since the aspiration to place oneself as high as possible in the university hierarchy, which is regarded as absolute, is what inspires the most sustained and efficacious scholastic endeavors. Adherence to the values implied in the academic hierarchy of performances is so strong that individuals can be seen to be drawn toward the school careers or competitions most highly valued by the educational system, independently of their personal aspirations or aptitudes. This is one of the factors in the otherwise often inexplicable attraction exerted by the *agrégation* and the *grandes écoles*, and more generally by abstract disciplines to which great prestige is attached. Perhaps it is the same principle that inclines French academics and intellectuals in general to assign the highest value to works in which the theoretical ambition is most manifest. Hence, the exclusion (at least in the eyes of academics) of the idea of a parallel hierarchy that would relativize the hierarchy of academic success, by enabling those at the very bottom to find excuses for themselves or to devalue the success of others.

In short, though it contradicts real justice by subjecting fundamentally unequal individuals to the same tests and the same criteria, the selection procedure which only takes account of performances measured by the academic criterion, other things being equal, is the only one appropriate to a system whose function is to produce selected, comparable individuals. But nothing in the logic of the system prevents allowance for real inequalities being brought into *the teaching itself*.

What might be called the charisma ideology (because it valorizes "grace" or the "gift") supplies the privileged classes with a

legitimation of their cultural privileges, which are thereby trans-
muted from a social heritage into individual grace or personal
merit. Behind this mask, "class racism" can be flaunted without
ever being seen for what it is. This alchemy succeeds all the better
inasmuch as, far from challenging it with an alternative image of
scholastic success, the working classes take over the essentialism
of the upper classes and experience their disadvantage as a personal destiny. It is universally acknowledged that a precocious
child is doubly gifted. However banal the flattery may seem, there
are weighty ethical implications in the admiring astonishment that
gratifies the fifteen-year-old *bachelier*, the "youngest *agrégé*," or
"France's youngest *polytechnicien*." And the innumerable stages
of the *cursus honorum* allow some individuals to perform the
miracle of eternal precocity, since it is always possible to become
the youngest member of the *Académie*. It is even in the most disadvantaged classes, where, traditionally, the social heredity of
abilities is strongly perceived—be they the craftsman's knack or
the tradesman's business sense—that one sometimes find the most
paradoxical expression of the charisma ideology. It is not uncommon for an interrupted schooling to be invoked, in the absence of
any success, to salvage the potentiality of the individual gift, by
the same logic by which the upper classes are able to point to
their gift actualized in their success.

Students are even more vulnerable to essentialism because, as
adolescents and apprentices, they are always in search of what
they *are,* so that what they *do* seems to concern their whole being.
As for the teachers who incarnate scholastic success and are required constantly to pass judgment on the abilities of others, their
professional ethic and morale depend on their regarding the abilities
they have more or less laboriously acquired as personal gifts and
on their imputing other people's acquired abilities and ability to
acquire abilities to their essential nature—the more so because
the educational system provides them with all the means of avoiding the self-conscious reflection that would lead them to question
themselves both as persons and as members of the cultivated
classes. Often originating from the lower middle class or from
teachers' families, they are all the more attached to the charisma
ideology which justifies arbitrary cultural privilege, because it
is only qua members of the intellectual class that they have some
share in the privileges of the bourgeoisie. Perhaps the reason why
the *agrégation* inspires such pugnacious champions is that it is one

of those privileges which can appear to be exclusively linked to personal merit and guaranteed by a procedure that (formally) is as democratic as can be.

Thus, nothing emerges to contradict the implicit ideology of the university and of university success, the exact opposite of a Kantian ethic of merit. All value is incarnated in the child prodigy, the brevity of whose path through school testifies to the extent of his gift. And when it does appear, the intention of relativizing the scholastic hierarchy of achievements paradoxically arms itself with the denigration of effort: the pejorative nicknames "swot," "bookworm," "grey," and so on, belong to a charismatic ideology which opposes works to grace only in order to devalue them in the name of grace.

It becomes clearer why merely describing social differences and the educational inequalities which arise from them is no routine operation but is in itself a challenge to the principle on which the present system is based. The unmasking of cultural privilege destroys the justificatory ideology which enables the privileged classes, the main users of the educational system, to see their success as the confirmation of natural, personal gifts. Since the ideology of the gift is based essentially on blindness to social inequalities in schooling and culture, mere description of the relationship between academic success and social origin has a critical force. Because everything inclines them to judge their own results in terms of the charisma ideology, students from the lower classes regard what they do as a simple product of what they are, and their obscure foreboding of their social destiny only increases their chances of failure, by the logic of the self-fulfilling prophecy. The essentialism implicitly contained in the charisma ideology thus reinforces the pressure of social determinisms. Because it is not perceived as linked to a certain social situation, for example, the intellectual atmosphere of the home, the structure of the language spoken there, or the attitude toward schooling and culture which it encourages, academic failure is naturally imputed to a lack of gifts. Children from the lower classes are indeed the appointed, consenting victims of the essentialist definitions in which clumsy teachers (disinclined, as we have seen, to relativize their own judgments sociologically) imprison individuals. When a pupil's mother says of her son, and often in front of him, "He's no good at French," she makes herself the accomplice of three sorts of damaging influences. First, unaware that her son's results are a direct function of the cultural atmosphere of his family background, she makes an individual destiny out of what is only the product of an education and can still be corrected, at least in part, by educative action. Secondly, for lack of information about schooling, sometimes for lack of anything to counterpose to the teachers' authority, she uses a simple test score as the basis for premature definitive conclusions. Finally, by sanctioning this type of judgment, she intensifies the child's sense that he is this or that by nature. Thus, the legitimatory authority of the school system can multiply social inequalities because the most disadvantaged classes, too conscious of their destiny and too unconscious of the ways in which it is brought about, thereby help to bring it upon themselves.

Because it always remains partial and patchy, perception of educational inequalities sometimes leads students to formulate diffuse demands which are only the inverted reflection of the casuistry by which, when deliberating on an examination, teachers make allowance, in their judgment, for this candidate's job in a boarding school, for that candidate's being an orphan, or for the fact that another has had polio. . . . Exceptions to the system here serve the logic of the system, with student pathos corresponding to professorial paternalism. Having ignored social handicaps all through the learning process (that is, when something could still have been done about them), teachers are prepared to discover them on examination day (but only as "special cases") because they then require no other remedy than generosity. In short, for students as for teachers, the immediate temptation could be to invoke social handicaps as an alibi or an excuse, that is, as a sufficient reason for suspending the formal requirements of the educational system. Another form of the same abdication, but a more dangerous one because it wields an apparent logic and flaunts the appearances of sociological relativism, is the populist illusion. This could lead students to demand that the parallel cultures of the disadvantaged classes should be given the status of the culture taught by the school system. But it is not sufficient to observe that school culture is a class culture; to proceed as if it were *only* that, is to help it remain so.

It is undeniable that some of the abilities demanded by the educational system, such as fluency in speech or writing and the very multiplicity of abilities, define and always will define learned culture. But the literature teacher is only entitled to expect the verbal and rhetorical virtuosity which appears to him, not un-reasonably, as associated with the very content of the culture he transmits, on condition that he sees this capacity for what it is, that is, as an aptitude that can be acquired through training, and that he undertakes to provide all his students with the means of acquiring it.

In the present state of society and of pedagogical traditions, the transmission of the techniques and habits of thought required by the school is first and foremost the work of the home environ-ment. Any real democratization, therefore, presupposes that these things be taught where the most disadvantaged can acquire them, that is, in school; that the area of what can be rationally and technically acquired by methodical learning be enlarged at the expense of what is irreducibly abandoned to the random distribu-tion of individual talents, that is, in fact, to the logic of social privileges; that the total, indivisible gifts in the charisma ideology be made available step by step through methodical teaching and learning. The educational interest of students from the most dis-advantaged classes, which is at present only expressed in the lan-guage of half-conscious, unconscious, or shamefaced behavior, would be to demand that their teachers "let the cat out of the bag," instead of staging an exemplary, inimitable show of prowess which masks the fact that grace is only a laborious acquirement or a social inheritance, and instead of supposing they have done their duty toward pedagogy for a whole year by handing over a few formulas that are discredited by their narrowly utilitarian aims (the notorious recipes for the dissertation) or devalued by the irony of transmitting them while accompanying them with magis-terial illustrations irreducible to their real usefulness. It would be too easy to assemble other examples of the bad faith which trans-forms the transmission of techniques into a ritual to the glory of professorial charisma, whether in terrifying, fascinating bibliog-raphies, exhortations to reading, writing, or research which are mere mockeries, or the professorial lecture which, because it can only address itself to students who are formally, fictitiously equal, is likely to combine every sort of pedagogic sham. But rational pedagogy is still to be invented, and can in no way be confused with the pedagogies we know at present, which, having only psy-chological foundations, in fact serve a system which does not and will not recognize social differences. So nothing is further from our minds than an appeal to so-called scientific pedagogy, which, while apparently increasing the formal rationality of teaching, would allow real inequalities to weigh more heavily than ever, with more justifications than ever. A truly rational pedagogy would have to be based on an analysis of the relative costs of the different modes of teaching (lectures, practicals, seminars, work groups) and the different types of pedagogic action by the teacher (from simple technical advice to actually directing students' work). It would have to take account of the content of the teaching or the vocational goals of the training, and, when considering the different types of pedagogic relation, it would have to bear in mind their differential efficiency according to students' social origins. In all cases, it would be dependent on the knowledge that is obtained of socially conditioned cultural inequality and on the decision to reduce it.

For example, of all the professorial duties, doubtless the one most regularly forgotten, both by certain teachers who have little interest in taking on an extra chore devoid of charm and prestige, and by certain students who would probably see it as intensifying the servitude in which they feel themselves to be held, is the continuous organization of exercises as an activity directed toward acquiring the material and intellectual techniques of intellectual work as completely and as quickly as possible. Tacit accomplices, teachers and students often agree on a definition of the tasks to be expected of teachers and students that involves the least effort for both of them. The teacher recognizes the student's freedom and pretends to see in him, all through the year, an independent or, more precisely, an autonomous worker, that is, one capable of disciplining himself, organizing his work, and keeping up a sustained, methodical, self-imposed effort. This is the price the teacher pays in order to receive from the student, whom he thus defines, the image he wishes to project and have of himself as a source of enlightenment, a *maître à penser* and not some pedagogue or college pedant—a quality teacher for quality students. Compulsory attendance at lectures or insistence on punctual submission of assignments would destroy both teacher and student as they see themselves and desire to be, as they see each other and desire each other to be.

Because the student cannot fail to have some sense of the requirements of all learning (namely, regular work or the discipline of exercises), he oscillates between the hankering for a tighter, more "scholastic" structuring of student life and the ideal, glamorous image of an aristocratic style of work, free of all control and discipline. And the same oscillations and ambivalence would be found in teachers' expectations. Thus, not infrequently a teacher who throughout the year puts forward the image of prowess and virtuosity judges his students' work by criteria quite different from those he seemed to suggest in his teaching, thereby showing that he could not possibly measure his own works and those of his students by the same standard. More generally, in the absence of a methodical enunciation of their principles and of any scientific approach to the practice of examining, professorial judgments are based on personal criteria, variable from teacher to teacher, and, like Weber's "Kadi-justice," remain directly tied to the particular case. Not surprisingly, students are usually forced to try to decipher the auguries and divine the secrets of the gods, with every chance of being wrong. It can be seen that there is no need to make explicit allowance for candidates' social handicaps in order to rationalize the examination and so to work toward rationalizing attitudes toward the examination, that sanctuary of irrationality. Students from the cultured classes are those best prepared (or least ill-prepared) to adapt themselves to a system of diffuse, implicit requirements, since they implicitly possess the means of satisfying those requirements. For example, by virtue of the clear affinity between school culture and the culture of the cultivated class, students from that class are able, in the personal encounter of the oral examination, to manifest those imponderable qualities which need not be consciously noticed by the examiner in order to enter into his judgment. The subconscious intuitions of class culture are the more insidious, in that conscious, explicit perception of social origin would be regarded as scandalous.

Thus, every step toward true rationality, whether in enunciation of the reciprocal requirements of teachers and taught, or in the organization of study best suited to enable students from the disadvantaged classes to overcome their disadvantages, would be a step toward equity. Students from the lower classes, who are the first to suffer from all the charismatic and traditional vestiges and who, more than others, are inclined to expect and demand everything from education, would be the first to benefit from an effort to give everyone the set of social "gifts" which constitute the reality of cultural privilege.

If it is accepted that truly democratic education is education which sets itself the unconditional goal of enabling *the greatest possible number of individuals to appropriate, in the shortest pos-*

sible time, as completely and as perfectly as possible, the greatest possible number of the abilities which constitute school culture at a given moment, then it is clear that it is opposed both to traditional education, which aims to train and select a well-born elite, and to technocratic education, aimed at mass production of made-to-measure specialists. But it is not sufficient to take as one's goal the true democratizing of education. In the absence of a rational pedagogy doing everything required to neutralize the effect of the social factors of cultural inequality, methodically and continuously, from kindergarten to university, the political project of giving everyone equal educational opportunity cannot overcome the real inequalities, even when it deploys every institutional and economic means. Conversely, a truly rational pedagogy, that is, one based on a sociology of cultural inequalities, would, no doubt, help to reduce inequalities in education and culture, but it would not be able to become a reality unless all the conditions for a true democratization of the recruitment of teachers and pupils were fulfilled, the first of which would be the setting up of a rational pedagogy.

Epilogue

ALICE LOOKED ROUND HER IN GREAT SUR-
prise. "Why, I do believe we've been under this tree the whole
time: Everything's just as it was!"

"Of course it is," said the Queen. "What would you have it?"

"Well, in *our* country," said Alice, still panting a little,
"you'd generally get to somewhere else—if you ran very fast for
a long time as we've been doing."

"A slow sort of country," said the Queen. "Now, *here,* you
see, it takes all the running you can do, to keep in the same place.
If you want to get somewhere else, you must run at least twice
as fast as that."

Lewis Carroll, *Through the Looking-*
Glass and What Alice Found There

Many of the recent changes in the educational system, the social
structure and the relationship between them, such as the "schooling
boom" (*l'explosion scolaire*) and the changed relationship between
formal qualifications and occupational hierarchies, are the result of
an intensified competition for academic qualifications. One important factor in intensifying this competition has doubtless been the
fact that those fractions of the dominant class and middle class who
are richest in economic capital (i.e., industrial and commercial em-
ployers, craftsmen, and tradesmen) have had to make greatly increased use of the educational system in order to ensure their social
reproduction. When class fractions who previously made little use
of the school system enter the race for academic qualifications, the
effect is to force the groups whose reproduction was mainly or exclusively achieved through education to step up their investments
so as to maintain the relative scarcity of their qualifications and,
consequently, their position in the class structure. Academic qualifications and the school system which awards them thus become
one of the key stakes in an interclass competition which generates

77

a general and continuous growth in the demand for education and an inflation of academic qualifications.[1]

Bearing in mind that the volume of corresponding jobs may also have varied over the same period, we may assume that a qualification is likely to have undergone devaluation if the number of diploma-holders has grown more rapidly than the number of suitable positions. Everything seems to suggest that the *baccalauréat* and lower qualifications are the ones most affected by such devaluation. To this must be added the less obvious devaluation resulting from the fact that if the number of corresponding jobs does keep pace, the positions themselves are likely to lose some of their scarcity value. This is what has happened, for example, to jobs at all levels of the teaching profession.

The very rapid growth in girls' and women's education has been a significant factor in the devaluing of academic qualifications. Because the image of the division of labor between the sexes has also changed, more women now bring academic qualifications onto the labor market which previously were partly held in reserve (and were "invested" only in the marriage market); and the higher the diploma, the more marked this growth has been. This shows, incidentally, that just as all segregation tends to slow down devaluation by its *numerus clausus* effect, so all desegregation tends to restore full strength to the devaluing mechanisms (and the least qualified are the ones who feel the effects most strongly).

It is no paradox to suggest that the chief victims of the devaluing of academic qualifications are those who enter the labor market without such qualifications. The devaluation of diplomas is accompanied by the gradual extension of the monopoly held by academic qualification holders over positions previously open to the academically unqualified, which has the effect of limiting the devaluation of qualifications by limiting the competition, but only at the cost of restricting the career opportunities available to the unqualified and of reinforcing the academic predetermination of the chances of an upward occupational trajectory. In statistical terms, there is a decline both in the dispersal of the holders of the same qualifications among different jobs and in the dispersal of the qualifications of holders of equivalent jobs, or in other words a reinforced correlation between academic qualification and job occupied.

It is clear that the market in jobs open to formally qualified candidates has grown constantly, inevitably at the expense of the formally unqualified. Universal recognition of academic qualifications no doubt has the effect of unifying the official set of qualifications for social positions and of eliminating local anomalies due to the existence of social spaces with their own rank-ordering principles. However, academic qualifications never achieve total, exclusive acceptance. Outside the specifically scholastic market, a diploma is worth what its holder is worth, economically and socially; the rate of return on educational capital is a function of the economic and social capital that can be devoted to exploiting it. Thus, the change in the distribution of posts among qualification-holders which results automatically from the increased number of formally qualified agents means that at every moment a proportion of the qualification-holders—starting, no doubt, with those who are least well endowed with the inherited means of exploiting their qualifications—are victims of devaluation. The strategies by which those who are most subject to devaluation endeavor to fight against it, in the short term (in the course of their own careers) or in the long term (through the strategies they employ for their children's schooling), are one of the decisive factors in the growth in the volume of qualifications awarded, which itself contributes to devaluation. The dialectic of devaluation and compensation thus tends to feed on itself.

Reproductive Strategies and Morphological Transformations

The strategies which individuals and families employ with a view to safeguarding or improving their position in social space are reflected in transformations which modify both the volume of the different class fractions and the structure of their assets. The reconversion of economic capital into academic capital is one of the strategies which enable the business bourgeoisie to maintain the position of some or all of its heirs, by enabling them to extract some of the profits of industrial and commercial firms in the form of salaries, which are a more discreet—and no doubt more reliable —mode of appropriation than "unearned" investment income. Thus, between 1954 and 1975 the proportion of industrialists and merchants fell sharply, whereas there was a very strong rise in the proportion of salary earners who owed their position to their academic qualifications—executives, engineers, teachers, and intellectuals (although, at least in the case of private-sector executives, a significant proportion of total income may be derived from shares). Similarly, the disappearance of many small commercial or craft firms conceals the reconversion work which individual agents perform, with varying degrees of success, in accordance with the demands of their particular situation, and which results in a transformation of the relative weight of the different fractions of the middle classes. Here, too, the decrease in the proportion of small shopkeepers, craftsmen, and farmers has been balanced by an increase in the proportion of primary-school teachers, technicians, and the personnel of the medical and social services. Furthermore, the relative morphological stability of an occupational group may conceal a transformation of its structure resulting from the reconversion *in situ* of agents present in the group at the beginning of the period (or their children) and/or their replacement by agents from other groups. For example, the relatively small decline in the overall volume of the category "shopkeepers," consisting very largely of the owners of small individual firms which have been able to withstand the crisis partly because of increased household consumption, conceals a change in the structure of this occupation. The stagnation or decline of small food stores, particularly hard hit by supermarket competition, and small clothing stores, has almost been balanced by a growth in the retailing of automobiles, domestic equipment (including furniture, interior decorating, and so on), and especially sports equipment, leisure goods, cultural commodities (books, records, and so on), and pharmaceuticals. These changes in the nature of retail firms—which are related to changes, over the same period, in the structure of household consumption, themselves related to the growth in incomes and above all to the increase in cultural capital resulting from the displacement of the structure of educational opportunity—are dialectically linked to a rise in the cultural capital of their owners or managers. Everything suggests that the "craftsman" category has undergone changes very similar to the "shopkeeper" category, with the decline of the most exposed strata of traditional craftsmanship being offset by the boom in luxury and "aesthetic" crafts, which require economic assets but also cultural capital. This would explain why the fall in the volume of these middle-class categories is accompanied by a rise in cultural capital as measured by educational level.

Craftsmen and tradesmen specializing in luxury, cultural, or artistic items, managers of fashion "boutiques," retailers of "famous maker" clothes, traders in exotic garments and jewels or rustic objects, record dealers, antique dealers, interior decorators, designers, photographers, restaurateurs, managers of trendy "bistros," Provençal "potters," avant-garde booksellers—all those seeking to prolong the fusion of leisure and work, militancy and dilettantism, that characterizes the student life-style—find that their ambiguous occupations, in which success depends at least as much on the subtly casual distinction of the vendor as on the nature and quality of his wares, are a way of obtaining the best return on a cultural capital in which technical competence is less important than familiarity with the culture of the dominant class and a mastery of the signs and emblems of distinction and taste. Because this new type of culture-intensive craftsmanship and retailing enables profit to be drawn from the cultural heritage transmitted directly by the family, it is predisposed to serve as a refuge for those sons and daughters of the dominant class who are eliminated by the educational system.

Time to Understand

The inflation of academic qualifications and the corresponding devaluation, which forces all social classes, starting with the greatest users of education, to make ever greater use of education and so in their turn to contribute to the overproduction of qualifications, have had a number of consequences. Undoubtedly the most important are the whole set of strategies whereby the holders of devalued qualifications have sought to maintain their inherited positions or to obtain from their qualifications the real equivalent of what those qualifications guaranteed in an earlier state of the relationship between diplomas and jobs.

We know that what an academic qualification guarantees is something much more than, and different from, the right to occupy a position and the capacity to perform the corresponding job. In this respect the diploma (*titre scolaire*) is more like a patent of nobility (*titre de noblesse*) than the title to property (*titre de propriété*) which strictly technical definitions make of it. So one can well understand that the holders of devalued qualifications are not inclined to perceive and acknowledge the devaluing of qualifications with which they are closely identified, both objectively (they constitute an important part of these people's social identity) and subjectively. But the concern to preserve self-esteem, which encourages attachment to the nominal value of qualifications and jobs, would not be sufficient to impose and maintain a misperception of this devaluation, if there was not also some complicity of objective mechanisms. The most important of these mechanisms are, first, the hysteresis of habitus,[2] which causes previously appropriate categories of perception and appreciation to be applied to a new state of the qualification market; and, second, the existence of relatively autonomous markets in which the value of academic qualifications declines at a slower rate.

The hysteresis effect is proportionately greater for agents who are more remote from the educational system and are poorly or only vaguely informed about the market in educational qualifications. One of the most valuable sorts of information constituting inherited cultural capital is practical or theoretical knowledge of the fluctuations of the market in academic qualifications, the eye for a good investment which enables one to get the best return on inherited cultural capital in the scholastic market or on scholastic capital in the labor market, for example by knowing the right moment to pull out of devalued disciplines and careers and to switch into ones with a future, rather than clinging to the scholastic values which secured the highest profits in an earlier state of the market. By contrast, the hysteresis effect means that the holders of devalued diplomas become, in a sense, accomplices in their own mystification, since, by a typical effect of *allodoxia*,[3] they bestow a value on their devalued diplomas which is not objectively acknowledged. This explains how those least informed about the diploma market, who have long been able to recognize a decline in real wages behind the maintenance of nominal wages, can continue to accept and seek the paper certificates which they receive in payment for their years of schooling, despite the fact that they are the ones most affected by diploma devaluation because of their lack of social capital.

This attachment to an anachronistic idea of the value of qualifications no doubt plays a part in the existence of markets in which diplomas can (apparently, at least) escape devaluation. The value objectively and subjectively placed on an academic qualification is in fact defined only by the totality of the social uses that can be made of it. Thus the evaluation of diplomas by one's direct acquaintance groups, such as relatives, neighbors, fellow students (one's "class" or "year"), and colleagues, can play an important role in masking the effects of devaluation. These phenomena of individual and collective misperception are in no way illusory, since they can in fact orient practices, especially the individual and collective strategies aimed at establishing or reestablishing the objective reality of the value of the qualification or position; and these strategies may make a real contribution toward actual re-valuation.

We know that in the transactions in which the market value of academic qualifications is defined, the strength of the vendors of labor power depends—setting aside their social capital—on the value of their diplomas, especially when the relationship between qualifications and jobs is strictly codified (as is the case with established positions, as opposed to new ones). So it is clear that the devaluation of academic diplomas is of direct advantage to the suppliers of jobs, and that, while the interests of qualification-holders are bound up with the nominal value of qualifications, i.e., with what they guaranteed by right in the earlier situation, the interests of job suppliers are bound up with the real value of quali-fications, in others words the value that is determined at the moment in question in the competition among the candidates. (This is a structural deskilling [*déqualification*] which aggravates the effects of the deskilling strategies which firms have been using for a long time.) The greatest losers in this struggle are those whose diplomas have least relative value in the hierarchy of diplomas and are most devalued. In some cases the qualification-holder finds he has no other way to defend the value of his qualification than to refuse to sell his labor power at the price offered; the decision to remain unemployed is then equivalent to a one-man strike.

The Bamboozling of a Generation

In a period of "diploma inflation," the disparity between the aspirations that the educational system produces and the oppor-tunities it really offers is a *structural* reality which affects all the members of a school generation, but to a varying extent depending on the rarity of their qualifications and on their social origins. New-comers to the educational system are led, by the mere fact of hav-ing access to it, to expect it to give them what it gave others at a time when they themselves were still excluded from it. In an earlier period and for another public, these aspirations were perfectly realistic, since they corresponded to objective probabilities, but they are often belied, with greater or lesser rapidity, by the verdicts of the scholastic market or the labor market. One of the great para-doxes of what is called the "democratization of schooling" is that only when the working classes, who had previously ignored or at best vaguely concurred in the ideology of "schooling as a liberatory force" (*l'école libératrice*), actually entered secondary education, did they discover *l'école conservatrice*, schooling as a conservative force, by being relegated to second-class courses or eliminated. The collective disillusionment which results from the structural mismatch between aspirations and real probabilities, between the social identity the school system seems to promise—or the one it offers on a temporary basis, that of "student," in the very wide sense the word has in popular usage, of someone placed for a certain time outside the necessities of the world of work—and the social identity that the labor market in fact offers is the source of that disaffection from work, that refusal of social finitude, which generates all the refusals and negations of the adolescent "counterculture."

This discrepancy—and the disenchantment it engenders—doubtless takes forms that are objectively and subjectively different in the various social classes. Thus, for working-class youngsters, the transit through secondary schooling produces misfirings of the dialectic of aspirations and probabilities which previously led them to accept their social destiny, almost always unquestioningly, and sometimes with positive eagerness (like the miners' sons who used to identify their entry into manhood with their first descent into the mine). The disenchantment with their work that is felt and expressed particularly acutely by the obvious victims of downclassing, such as *baccalauréat*-holders obliged to take jobs as factory workers or postmen, is, in a way, common to a whole generation. It finds expression in unusual forms of struggle, protest, and escapism that the organizations traditionally involved in industrial or political struggle find hard to understand, because something more and other than the worker's "situation" is at issue. These young people, whose social identity and self-image have been undermined by a social system and an educational system that have fobbed them off with worthless paper, can find no other way of restoring their personal and social integrity than by a total refusal. It is as if they felt that what is at issue is no longer just a question of personal failure, as the educational system encourages them to believe, but rather the whole logic of the academic institution. The structural deskilling of a whole generation, who are bound to get less out of their qualifications than the previous generation would have obtained, engenders a sort of collective disillusionment: a whole generation, finding it has been taken for a ride, is inclined to extend to all institutions the mixture of revolt and resentment it feels toward the educational system. This anti-institutional cast of mind (which draws strength from ideological and scientific critiques) can lead in extreme cases to a denunciation of the social order, a practical suspension of doxic adherence to the prizes it offers and the values it professes, and a withholding of the investments which are a necessary condition of its functioning.

So it is understandable that, not only within families but also in educational institutions and political or union organizations, and above all in the work situation, whenever old-style autodidacts, who started out thirty years earlier with a *certificat d'études* or a BEPC[4] and boundless respect for culture, come into contact with young holders of the *baccalauréat* or a university diploma, or new-style autodidacts, who bring their anti-institutional stance with them into the institution, the clash of generations often takes the form of a showdown over the very foundations of the social order. More radical and also more uncertain of its own ground than the usual form of political contestation, and reminiscent of the mood of the first Romantic generation, this disenchanted temperament attacks the fundamental tenets of the petit-bourgeois order—"career," "status," "promotion," "grade," and so on.

Whereas in 1962 only 1.5 per cent of semiskilled workers aged between 15 and 24 had the BEPC, and 0.2 per cent the *baccalauréat* or a higher degree, in 1975 the corresponding percentages were 8.2 and 1.0 (the figures for semiskilled workers aged over 55 remained very low—1.7 per cent and 0.5 per cent respectively in 1975). Among white-collar workers, where there was a relatively high percentage of diploma-holders even in 1962 and even among older workers, the proportion of the very highly qualified rose faster among the young, so that by 1975 a larger proportion of them had high qualifications than of older workers (in 1962, 25.0 per cent of office workers aged 15 to 24 had the BEPC, 2.0 per cent the *baccalauréat,* and 0.2 per cent a higher education degree, compared with 38.0 per cent, 8.0 per cent and 1.0 per cent in 1975; the corresponding figures for older staff were 16.1 per cent, 3.3 per cent and 1.4 per cent). In addition to all the changes in the relations between colleagues of different generations that are implied in these statistics, we have to bear in mind the changed relation to work which results from putting agents with higher qualifications into jobs that are often deskilled (by automation and all the forms of job mechanization which have turned white-collar staff into the production-line workers of the great bureaucracies). There is every reason to think that the opposition between the somewhat strict and even stuffy rigor of the older staff, and the casual style of the younger workers, which is doubtless perceived as sloppiness especially when it includes long hair and a beard, the traditional emblems of the bohemian artist or intellectual, expresses rather more than a simple generation gap or a change in cosmetic or clothing fashions.

The Struggle against Downclassing

The strategies agents use to avoid the devaluation of their diplomas—of which only the most visible ones are generally noticed, i.e., the collective strategies by which a dominated group endeavors to maintain or increase the advantages it has won—are thus grounded in the discrepancy between opportunities objectively available at any given moment and aspirations based on an earlier structure of objective opportunities. This discrepancy, which is particularly acute at certain moments and in certain social positions, generally reflects a failure to achieve the individual or collective occupational trajectory which was inscribed as an objective potentiality in the former position and in the trajectory leading to it. When this "broken trajectory" effect occurs—for example the case of a man whose father and grandfather were *polytechniciens* and who becomes a sales engineer or a psychologist, or the case of a law graduate who, for lack of social capital, becomes a community cultural worker—the agent's aspirations, flying on above his real trajectory like a projectile carried on by its own inertia, describe an ideal trajectory that is no less real or is at any rate in no way imaginary, in the ordinary sense of the word. This impossible objective potentiality, inscribed at the deepest level of their dispositions as a sort of blighted hope or frustrated promise, is the factor that can unite those sons and daughters of the bourgeoisie to whom the educational system has not given the means of pursuing the trajectory most likely for their class, and those sons and daughters of the petite bourgeoisie who have not obtained the rewards which their academic qualifications would have guaranteed in an earlier state of the market—two categories who are particularly likely to try to move into new positions.

Agents who seek to avoid downclassing can either produce new occupations more closely matching their pretensions (which were socially justified in an earlier state of relations between qualifications and jobs), or refurbish the occupations to which their qualifications do give access, redefining and upgrading them in accordance with their pretensions.[5] When agents start to arrive in a job who possess qualifications different from those of the usual occupants, they bring hitherto unknown aptitudes, dispositions, and demands with them into their relation with that job, in terms both of its technical definition and its social definition; and this necessarily causes changes in the job itself. Among the most visible changes observed when the newcomers have high qualifications are an intensified division of labor, with autonomous status being given to some of the tasks previously performed, in principle or in practice, by less qualified jacks-of-all-trades (e.g., the diversification of the education and social welfare fields); and, often, a redefinition of careers, related to the emergence of expectations and demands that are new both in form and content. There is every reason to suppose that the job redefinition resulting from a change in the scholastic properties of the occupants—and all their associated properties—is likely to be more or less extensive depending on the elasticity of the technical and social definition of the position (which is probably greater at higher levels in the hierarchy of positions) and on the social origin of the new occupants, since the higher their origin, the less inclined they will be to accept the limited ambitions of petit-bourgeois agents looking for modest, predictable progress over a lifetime. These factors are probably not independent. Whether led by their sense of a good investment and their awareness of the opportunities awaiting their capital, or by the refusal to demean themselves by entering one of the established occupations whose transparent significance makes them invidious, those sons and daughters of the bourgeoisie who are threatened with downclassing tend to move, if they possibly can, into the most indeterminate of the older professions and into the sectors where the new professions are under construction. This "creative redefinition" is therefore found particularly in the most ill-defined and professionally unstructured occupations and in the newest sectors of cultural and artistic production, such as the big public and private organizations engaged in cultural production (radio, TV, marketing, advertising, social science research, and so on), where jobs and careers have not yet acquired the rigidity of the older bureaucratic professions and recruitment is generally done by cooption, i.e., on the basis of "connections" and affinities of habitus, rather than formal qualifications. This means that the sons and daughters of the Paris bourgeoisie, rather than directly entering a well-defined and lifelong profession (e.g., teaching), are more likely to enter and to succeed in positions, halfway between studenthood and a profession, that are offered by the big cultural bureaucracies, occupations for which the specific qualifications (e.g., a diploma in filmmaking, or a sociology or psychology degree) are a genuine ticket of entry only for those who are able to supplement the official qualifications with the real—social—qualifications.

But the site *par excellence* of this type of transformation is found in the group of occupations whose common factor is that they ensure a maximum return on that aspect of cultural capital which is embodied in good manners, good taste, or even bearing and physical charm—products of the internalization of the bodily norms prevailing in the dominant class which are directly transmitted by the family and so do not depend on scholastic inculcation and consecration. This group includes the aesthetic and semi-aesthetic, intellectual and semi-intellectual occupations, but also all the various consultancy services (psychology, vocational guidance, speech therapy, beauty advice, marriage counseling, diet workshops, and so on), the educational and paraeducational occupations (youth leaders, runners of daycare centers, cultural program organizers) and jobs involving presentation and representation (tour organizers, hostesses, cicerones, couriers, radio and TV announcers, news anchors, and quiz show hosts, press attachés, public relations people, and so on).

Public and, especially, private bureaucracies are now obliged to perform representational and "hosting" functions which are very different in both scale and style from those traditionally entrusted to men (diplomats, ministerial attachés, and so on, often drawn from those fractions of the dominant class—the aristocracy and the old bourgeoisie—who were richest in social capital and in the socializing techniques essential to the maintenance of that capital). The new requirements have led to the emergence of a whole set of female occupations and to the establishment of a legitimate market in physical properties. The fact that certain women derive occupational profit from their charm(s), and that beauty thus acquires a value on the labor market, has doubtless helped to produce not only a number of changes in the norms of clothing and cosmetics, but also a whole set of changes in ethics and a redefinition of the traditional image of femininity. Women's magazines and all the acknowledged authorities on the body and the legitimate ways to use it transmit the image of womanhood incarnated by these professional manipulators of bureaucratic charm, who are rationally

selected and trained, in accordance with a strictly programed ca-
reer-structure (with specialized schools, beauty contests, and so
on), to fulfill the most traditional feminine functions in conformity
with bureaucratic norms.

The most indeterminate sectors of the social structure offer the
most favorable ground for the operations which, by transforming
old positions or "creating" new ones *ex nihilo,* aim to produce
areas of specialist expertise, particularly in the field of "consultancy," the performance of which requires no competence more
specific than competence in a class culture. The constitution of a
socially recognized corps of experts specializing in advice on sex-
uality, which is now coming about through the gradual profession-
alization of voluntary, philanthropic, or political associations, is the
paradigmatic form of the process whereby agents tend, with that
inner sense of disinterestedness which is the basis of all missionary
zeal, to satisfy their "categorial" interests by deploying the quan-
tum of legitimate culture with which they have been endowed by
the educational system so as to accredit themselves in the eyes of
the classes excluded from legitimate culture, thereby ensuring the
need for and the rarity of their class culture. It goes without saying
that, here as elsewhere, the responsibility for the change cannot be
imputed to this or that agent or class of agents working with self-
interested lucidity or disinterested conviction to create the necessary conditions for the success of their undertaking. From marriage
counselors to the vendors of reducing aids, all those who now make
a profession of supplying the means of bridging the gap between
"is" and "ought" in the realm of the body and its uses would be
nothing without the unconscious collusion of all those who contribute to producing an inexhaustible market for the products they
offer, who by imposing new uses of the body and a new bodily
hexis[6]—the *hexis* which the new bourgeoisie of the sauna bath, the
gymnasium and the ski slope has discovered for itself—produce the
corresponding needs, expectations, and dissatisfactions. Doctors
and diet experts armed with the authority of science, who impose
their definition of normality with height-weight tables, balanced
diets, or models of sexual adequacy; couturiers who confer the
sanction of good taste on the unattainable measurements of fashion
models; advertisers for whom the new obligatory uses of the body
provide scope for countless warnings and reminders ("Watch your
weight!" "Someone isn't using . . ."); journalists who exhibit and
glorify their own life-style in women's magazines and magazines

for well-heeled executives—all combine, in the competition between them, to advance a cause which they can serve so well only
because they are not always aware of serving it or even of serving
themselves in the process. And the emergence of this new petite
bourgeoisie, which employs new means of manipulation to perform
its role as an intermediary between the classes and which by its
very existence brings about a transformation of the position and
dispositions of the old petite bourgeoisie, can itself be understood
only in terms of changes in the mode of domination, which, substituting seduction for repression, public relations for armed force,
advertising for authority, the velvet glove for the iron fist, pursues
the symbolic integration of the dominated classes by imposing
needs rather than inculcating norms.

Compensatory Strategies

The specific contradiction in the scholastic mode of reproduction lies in the opposition between the interests of the class which
the educational system serves statistically and the interests of those
members of the class whom it sacrifices, i.e., the so-called failures
who are threatened with downclassing for lack of the qualifications
formally required of rightful members. This is not to mention those
holders of qualifications which "normally"—i.e., in an earlier state
of the relationship between diplomas and jobs—gave access to a
bourgeois occupation, who, because they do not originate from
that class, lack the social capital to extract the full yield from their
academic qualifications. The overproduction of qualifications, and
the consequent devaluation, tend to become a structural constant
when theoretically equal chances of obtaining qualifications are
offered to all the offspring of the bourgeoisie (regardless of birth-
rank or sex) while the access of other classes to these qualifications
also increases (in absolute terms). The strategies which one group
employs to try to escape downclassing and to return to their class
trajectory, and which the other group employs to rebuild the interrupted path of a hoped-for trajectory, are today one of the most
important factors in the transformation of social structures. The
individual "catching-up" strategies which enable the holders of a
social capital of inherited "connections" to make up for their lack
of formal qualifications or to get the maximum return from those
they have managed to obtain, by moving into relatively unbureau-
cratized areas of social space (where social dispositions count for
more than academically guaranteed "competences"), are com-

bined with collective strategies aimed at asserting the value of formal qualifications and obtaining the rewards they secured in an earlier state of the market. The combined effect is to encourage the creation of a large number of semibourgeois positions, produced by redefining old positions or inventing new ones, and designed to save unqualified "inheritors" from downclassing and to provide "parvenus" with an approximate equivalent for their devalued qualifications.

An analysis of these compensatory strategies is sufficient to show how naive it would be to see a merely mechanical process of inflation and devaluation at work. The massive increase in the school population has caused a whole set of transformations both inside and outside the educational system, modifying its organization and operation partly through morphological transformations at all its levels but also through defensive manoeuvres by its traditional users, such as the multiplication of subtly ranked paths through it and skilfully disguised "dumping-grounds" which help to blur perception of its hierarchies. For the sake of clarity, we may contrast two states of the French secondary school system. In the older state, the organization of the institution, the pathways it offered, the courses it taught, and the qualifications it awarded were all based on sharp divisions, clear-cut boundaries; the primary/secondary division produced systematic differences in all dimensions of the culture taught, the teaching methods used, and the careers promised. In the present state of the system, the exclusion of the great mass of working-class and lower-middle-class children takes place not at the moment of entry into *sixième,*[7] but steadily and impalpably, all through the first years of secondary schooling, through hidden forms of elimination such as repeated years (equivalent to a deferred elimination); relegation into second-class courses, entailing a stigmatization that tends to induce proleptic recognition of scholastic and social destiny; and finally the awarding of devalued certificates.

Whereas the old system with its strongly marked boundaries led to the internalizing of scholastic divisions clearly corresponding to social divisions, the new system with its fuzzy classifications and blurred edges encourages and entertains (at least among the new "intermediaries" in social space) aspirations that are themselves blurred and fuzzy. Aspiration levels are now adjusted to scholastic hurdles and standards in a less strict and also a less harsh manner than under the old system, which was characterized by the remorseless rigor of the national competitive examination. It is true that the new system fobs off a good number of its users with devalued qualifications, playing on the faulty perceptions that are encouraged by the anarchic profusion of courses and diplomas that are difficult to compare and yet subtly ranked in prestige. However, it does not force them into such abrupt "disinvestment" as the old system: the blurring of hierarchies and boundaries between the elected and the rejected, between true and false qualifications, plays a part in "cooling out" and in calm acquiescence in being cooled out. The new system favors the development of a less realistic, less resigned relationship to the future than the old sense of proper limits, which was the basis of an acute sense of hierarchy. The *allodoxia*[8] which the new system encourages in innumerable ways is the reason why relegated agents collaborate in their own relegation by overestimating the studies on which they embark, overvaluing their qualifications, and banking on possible futures which do not really exist for them; but it is also the reason why they do not truly accept the objective reality of their position and qualifications. And the reason for the attractiveness of the new or potentially renewable positions lies in the fact that, being vague and ill-defined, uncertainly located in social space, often offering (like the occupations of "artist" or "intellectual" in the past) none of the material or symbolic criteria —promotion, benefits, increments—whereby *social time,* and also social hierarchies, are experienced and measured, they leave aspirations considerable room for manoeuvre. They thus make it possible to avoid the sudden, final disinvestment imposed by occupations that are clearly delimited and defined from recruitment to retirement. The indeterminate future which they offer, a privilege hitherto reserved for artists and intellectuals, makes it possible to treat the present as a sort of endlessly renewed provisional status and to regard one's "station" as an accidental detour, like the painter who works in advertising but continues to consider himself a "true" artist and insists that this mercenary trade is only a temporary expedient that will be abandoned as soon as he has put by enough money to be independent. These ambiguous occupations exempt their practitioners from the work of disinvestment and reinvestment that is implied, for example, in switching from a "vocation" as a philosopher to a "vocation" as a philosophy teacher, or from artist to publicity designer or art teacher—or at least allow them to defer their transfer indefinitely. It is not surprising that such people should be drawn to schemes of "continuing education" (*l'éducation permanente*), to permanent presence in the educational system, which offers an open, unlimited future and contrasts diametrically with the system of national competitions designed to demonstrate, once and for all, and as early as possible, that what is done cannot be undone. Again, it is understandable that, like artists, they should so readily embrace the aesthetic and ethical modes and models of youth: it is a way of showing to oneself and others that one is not finite, finished, defined. In place of abrupt, all-or-nothing breaks, between study and work, between work and retirement, there is an impalpable, infinitesimal sliding (consider all the temporary or semipermanent occupations, often occupied by students approaching the end of their course, which cluster around the established positions in scientific research or higher education or, in another sphere, consider the phased retirement now offered by the most "advanced" firms). Everything takes place as if the new logic of the educational system and economic system encouraged people to defer for as long as possible the moment of ultimate crystallization toward which all the infinitesimal changes point, in other words the final balance sheet which sometimes takes the form of a "personal crisis." It goes without saying that the adjustment between objective chances and subjective aspirations that is thereby established is both more subtle and more subtly extorted, but also more risky and unstable. Maintaining vagueness in the images of the present and future of one's position is a way of accepting limits, but it is also a way to avoid acknowledging them or, to put it another way, a way of refusing them. But it is a refusal in bad faith, the product of an ambiguous cult of revolution which springs from resentment at the disappointment of imaginary expectations. Whereas the old system tended to produce clearly demarcated social identities which left little room for fantasy but were comfortable and reassuring even in the unconditional renunciation which they demanded, the new system of structural instability in the representation of social identity and its legitimate aspirations tends to shift agents from the terrain of social crisis and criticism to the terrain of personal criticism and crisis.

Competitive Struggles and Displacement of the Structure

It can be seen how naive it is to claim to settle the question of "social change" by locating "newness" or "innovation" in a particular site in social space. For some, this site is at the top; for others, at the bottom; and it is always *elsewhere,* in all the "new," "marginal," "excluded," or "dropped-out" groups, for all those sociologists whose chief concern is to bring "newness" into the discussion at all costs. But to characterize a class as "conservative" or "innovating" (without even specifying in what respect it is so), by tacit recourse to an ethical standard which is necessarily situated socially, produces a discourse which states little more than the site from which it is produced, because it sweeps aside what is essential, namely the field of struggles, the system of objective relations within which positions and postures are defined *relationally* and which governs even those struggles aimed at transforming it. Only by reference to the space in the game which defines them and which they seek to maintain or redefine, more or less comprehensively, *as* a space in the game, can one understand the strategies, individual or collective, spontaneous or organized, which are aimed at conserving, transforming, transforming so as to conserve, or even conserving so as to transform.

Reconversion strategies are nothing other than an aspect of the permanent actions and reactions whereby each group strives to maintain or change its position in the social structure, or, more precisely—at a stage in the evolution of class societies in which one can conserve only by changing—to change so as to conserve. Frequently the actions whereby each class (or class fraction) works to win new advantages, i.e., to gain an advantage over the other classes and so, objectively, to reshape the structure of objective relations between the classes (the relations revealed by the statistical *distributions* of properties), are compensated for (and so canceled out *ordinally*) by the reactions of the other classes, directed toward the same objective. In this particular (though very common) case, the outcome of these opposing actions, which cancel each other out by the very countermovements which they generate, is an overall displacement of the structure of the distribution, between the classes or class fractions, of the assets at stake in the competition (as has happened in the case of the chances of university entrance).

A similar process of homothetic development seems to take place whenever the strengths and efforts of the groups competing for a determinate type of asset or entitlement tend to balance one another out in a race in which, after a series of scrambles in which various groups forge ahead or catch up, the initial gaps are maintained; in other words, whenever the attempts of the initially most disadvantaged groups to come into possession of the assets or entitlements previously possessed by groups immediately above them in the social hierarchy or immediately ahead of them in the race are more or less counterbalanced, at all levels, by the efforts of better-placed groups to maintain the scarcity and distinctiveness of their assets or entitlements. One thinks of the struggle which the sale of letters of nobility provoked among the English aristocracy in the second half of the sixteenth century, triggering a self-sustaining process of inflation and devaluation of these titles. The lowest titles, such as esquire or arms, were the first to be affected, followed by the rank of knight, which was devalued so fast that the oldest holders had to press for the creation of a new title, that of baronet. But this new title, which filled the gap between knight and peer of the realm, was seen as a threat by the holders of the higher rank, whose value depended on a certain distance.[9] With academic titles as with titles of nobility, newcomers objectively strive to devalue the existing holders by taking possession of the titles which made them rare: the surest way to devalue a title of nobility is to purchase it as a commoner. The existing holders, for their part, objectively devalue the newcomers either by abandoning their titles to them in order to pursue rarer ones, or by introducing differences among the title-holders linked to seniority in accession to the title (such as the manner of possessing it). It follows that all the groups involved in the race, whatever rank they occupy, cannot conserve their position, their rarity, their rank, except by running to keep their distance from those immediately behind them, thus jeopardizing the difference which distinguishes the group immediately in front; or, to put it another way, by aspiring to possess that which the group just ahead already have, and which they *will* have, but later.

The dialectic of downclassing and upclassing which underlies a whole set of social processes presupposes and entails that all the groups concerned run in the same direction, toward the same objectives, the same properties, those which are designated by the leading group and which, by definition, are unavailable to the groups following, since, whatever these properties may be intrinsically, they are modified and qualified by their distinctive rarity and will no longer be what they were, once they are multiplied and made available to groups lower down. Thus, by an apparent paradox, the maintenance of order, i.e., of the whole set of gaps, differences, "differentials," ranks, precedences, priorities, exclusions, distinctions, ordinal properties, and thus of the relations of

order which give a social formation its structure, is provided by an
unceasing change in substantial (i.e., nonrelational) properties.
This implies that the social order established at any given moment
is also necessarily a temporal order, an "order of successions" as
Leibniz put it, each group having as its past the group immediately
below and for its future the group immediately above (one sees the
attraction of evolutionist models). The competing groups are separated by differences whch are essentially located in the order of
time. The dialectic of downclassing and upclassing is predisposed
to function also as an ideological mechanism whose effects conservative discourse strives to intensify: especially when they compare their present conditions with their past, or resort to credit to
satisfy their impatience for immediate enjoyment, the stragglers in
the race are exposed to the illusion that they have only to wait in
order to receive advantages which, in reality, they will obtain only
by struggle. By situating the difference between the classes in the
order of successions, the competitive struggle establishes a difference which, like that which separates predecessor from successor
in a social order governed by well-defined rules of succession, is
not only the most absolute and unbridgeable (since there is nothing
to do but wait, sometimes a whole lifetime like the petit-bourgeois
who acquire their own houses at the moment of retirement, sometimes several generations like the petit-bourgeois who extend their
own foreshortened trajectories through their children), but also
the most unreal and evanescent (since a person knows that if he
can wait, he will in any case get what he is promised by the in-
eluctable laws of evolution). In short, what the competitive struggle
makes everlasting is not different positions, but the difference between positions.

To understand this mechanism means, first of all, to perceive the
futility of the abstract debates which arise from the opposition of
permanence and change, structure and history, reproduction and
the "production of society." The real basis of such debates is the
refusal to acknowledge that social contradictions and struggles are
not all, or always, in contradiction with the perpetuation of the
established order; that, beyond the antitheses of "thinking in
couples," permanence can be ensured by change and the structure
perpetuated by movement. It also becomes clear that those who
point to what might be called "cardinal" properties and speak of
the *"embourgeoisement"* of the working class, and those who try
to refute them by pointing to ordinal properties, have in common

an unawareness that the contradictory aspects of reality which they isolate are in fact indissoluble dimensions of a single reality. The reproduction of the social structure can take place in and through a competitive struggle leading to a simple displacement of the structures of distributions, so long and only so long as the members of the dominated classes enter the struggle in extended order, i.e., through actions and reactions which are compounded only *statistically,* by the *external effects* which the actions of some exert on the actions of others, in the absence of any interaction or transaction, and consequently in conditions of objectivity, without collective or individual control and generally against the agents' individual and collective interests.[10] Competitive struggle is the form of class struggle which the dominated classes allow to be imposed on them when they accept the stakes offered by the dominant classes. It is an *integrative* struggle and, by virtue of the initial handicaps, a *reproductive* struggle, since those who enter this chase, in which they are beaten before they start as the constancy of the gaps testifies, implicitly recognize the legitimacy of the goals pursued by those whom they pursue, by the mere fact of taking part.

Having established the logic of the processes of competition (or rout) which condemn each agent to react in isolation to the effect of the countless reactions of other agents or, more precisely, to the result of the statistical aggregation of their isolated actions, and which reduce the class to the state of a mass dominated by its own number, we are able to pose the question, much debated at present among historians,[11] of the conditions (economic crisis, economic crisis following a period of expansion, and so on) in which the dialectic of mutually self-reproducing objective chances and subjective aspirations may break down. Everything suggests that an abrupt slump in objective chances relative to subjective aspirations is likely to produce a break in the tacit acceptance which the dominated classes—now abruptly excluded from the race, objectively and subjectively—previously granted to the dominant goals, and so to make it possible to invent or impose the goals of a genuine collective action.

Appendixes

1·Students
in France
Statistical Data
1960–63[1]

The proportion of female students in the university population
rose from 6 percent in 1906 to 41.6 percent in 1962 (see fig. 1.1).
Apart from the peaks due to the two wars, the rise has been a
steady one.

In 1906, there were proportionately twice as many female
students in Paris as in the provinces, but by 1916 the gap was
insignificant, and since then, with a few irregularities, the most
important of which coincides with the 1939–45 war, female attendance at the universities has continued to rise at much the
same rate in Paris and the provinces. The slightly higher level in
Paris throughout this period may indicate that abandonment of
traditional models is more strongly resisted in the provinces. This
phenomenon is particularly apparent in the first phase of women's
entry into the universities, that is, before 1911. In 1962, women
made up 43 percent of the total student population in Paris and
41 percent in the provinces.

Contrary to the impression given by the growth in the number
of Parisian students (in university buildings that have remained virtually the same), Paris's share of the national student population
changed very little between 1900 and 1955, from 42.7 percent in
1900–1901 to 43.9 percent in 1950–51 (except for a sharp fall
due to the war and occupation); and then steadily declined, from
42.1 percent in 1955–56 to 32.5 percent in 1962–63 (39.2 percent
in 1957–58, 37.9 percent in 1958–59, 35.9 percent in 1959–60,
35.6 percent in 1960–61, 33.0 percent in 1961–62).

The overall ninefold increase in student numbers, from 29,759
in 1900–1901 to 266,556 in 1962–63, has been unequally re-

101

TABLE 1.1. Number of Students in Each University, 1901–63

Years Universities	Aix Marseilles	Besançon	Bordeaux	Caen	Clermont	Dijon	Grenoble	Lille
1900–01	950	252	2,119	803	299	669	566	1,209
1910–11	1,264	239	2,620	794	278	1,043	1,272	1,893
1915–16	482	80	948	291	135	240	587	64
1920–21	1,596	266	2,640	1,055	467	744	2,737	1,475
1925–26	1,971	458	3,000	1,180	621	1,015	2,931	2,420
1930–31	2,988	571	4,254	1,828	1,077	1,397	3,197	3,748
1935–36	3,169	451	3,932	1,317	1,025	1,047	2,180	3,221
1940–41	5,550	388	3,657	1,832	2,014	864	3,560	2,475
1945–46	5,496	745	6,242	2,624	2,007	1,172	3,954	6,225
1950–51	7,556	933	8,147	3,083	2,108	1,820	4,199	6,382
1955–56	9,679	1,157	9,511	3,826	2,758	2,426	4,685	7,406
1960–61[a]	15,486	2,217	12,267	6,357	4,731	3,706	10,007	11,503
1961–62	19,020	2,889	13,805	7,395	5,556	4,578	10,471	13,101
1962–63[b]	22,160	3,361	16,440	8,478	6,028	5,254	12,951	14,612
Between 1901 and 1963 the number of students was multiplied by	23	13	8	11	20	8	23	12

a. From 1960–61, the numbers include all the students attending the universities, that is, those enrolled in the faculties plus those not enrolled but belonging to establishments connected either to the universities or the faculties.

b. The 1962–63 figures are provisional: the final figures will be slightly higher.

c. In 1961–62 and 1962–63 the total also includes the students in the universities of Nantes, Orléans, and Reims, 7,147 in 1961–62 and 8,417 in 1962–63.

Lyon	Mont-pellier	Nancy	Paris	Poitiers	Rennes	Stras-bourg	Tou-louse	Total
2,458	1,610	1,027	12,381	1,028	1,609	—	2,040	29,020
3,091	2,028	1,886	17,326	1,314	1,995	—	2,864	39,907
881	654	356	5,522	428	651	—	825	12,144
3,409	2,615	2,002	21,232	1,238	1,946	—	2,680	48,517
3,575	2,428	2,554	25,123	1,578	1,929	2,889	3,171	56,843
4,965	3,810	4,287	31,886	2,107	2,850	3,255	4,370	76,590
4,998	3,126	3,105	32,577	1,969	2,647	2,760	4,016	71,250
6,695	4,900	1,158	23,352	2,626	4,207	2,543	6,894	72,715
6,958	5,091	3,894	53,427	3,118	5,032	4,520	7,665	118,170
7,865	5,685	4,602	58,958	4,127	6,343	5,069	7,531	134,408
9,258	7,054	5,231	64,151	4,546	7,161	5,343	8,054	152,246
13,315	10,509	8,294	77,796	6,843	11,092	8,479	12,070	214,672
15,351	13,361	8,682	81,617	6,310	9,253	11,686	14,592	244,814c
17,230	15,802	9,830	90,354	7,412	9,323	12,444	16,752	276,848c
7	10	9	7	7	6	—	8	9

TABLE 1.2.   Number of Female Students in Paris and Provinces

Academic Years	Paris			Provinces			Combined		
	Total	Women	% W	Total	Women	% W	Total	Women	% W
1905–06	14,734	1,231	8.3	18,582	657	3.5	33,316	1,988	9.6
1910–11	17,326	2,121	12.2	23,864	1,833	7.7	41,190	3,954	14.7
1915–16	5,522	1,447	26.2	7,044	1,761	25.0	12,566	3,208	25.8
1920–21	21,232	3,200	15.1	28,195	4,100	14.5	49,727	7,300	6.0
1925–26	25,123	5,445	21.7	33,119	6,787	20.5	58,242	12,232	25.5
1930–31	31,886	8,487	26.6	46,438	11,701	25.2	78,324	20,188	21
1935–36	32,577	9,251	28.4	41,201	11,030	26.8	73,778	20,281	27.5
1940–41	23,352	9,020	38.6	49,963	15,811	32	72,715	24,831	34.1
1945–46	53,427	18,357	34.3	67,488	20,268	31.4	117,915	38,625	32.7
1950–51	58,958	20,227	35.3	75,135	25,384	33.8	134,093	43,611	34
1955–56	64,151	23,638	36.8	88,095	31,752	36.5	152,246	55,390	36.4
1960–61	72,449	31,028	42.8	130,926	52,540	40.1	203,375	83,568	41.1
1961–62	76,707	32,882	42.9	155,903	63,932	41	232,610	96,814	41.6

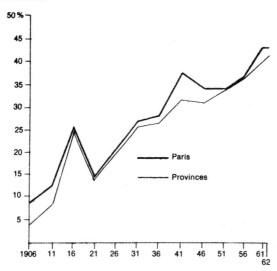

Fig. 1.1. Percentage of Female Students, in Paris and Provinces, from 1906 to 1962

flected in the various faculties. The number of students in Pharmacy faculties has tripled, from 3,347 in 1901 to 10,174 in 1962–63. Over the same period, the number of Law students, rising from 10,152 to 45,511, has increased fourfold, as has the number of Medical students (37,633 from 8,627). However, the growth has been more irregular in Law than in Medicine. Science and Arts have expanded side by side, despite some irregularities. Their numbers were multiplied by 23 between 1901 and 1963, Science students rising from 3,910 to 88,175, and Arts students from 3,723 to 85,063. Since 1956, the two curves have tended to merge. The slow growth of Law and Medicine is easily explained by the limited expansion in career outlets, whereas the fact that Arts subjects continue to grow as fast as the sciences must be partly attributed to cultural inertia.

Until 1945 the numbers are fairly similar in the different faculties and relatively stable (especially between 1921 and 1941); from then on there is an overall growth, very unequally distributed among the faculties. The growth rate of the student population has steadily risen since 1946, and the numbers have tripled during this period. As Raymond Aron has pointed out,[2] throughout western Europe, growth in the social demand for education preceded the rise in economic growth rate, which did not have a

TABLE 1.3. Number of Female Students in Each Discipline

Years	Law Total	Law Women	Science Total	Science Women	Arts Total	Arts Women	Medicine Total	Medicine Women	Pharmacy Total	Pharmacy Women	All Disciplines Total	All Disciplines Women
1900–01	10,152	16	3,910	98	3,723	243	8,627	508	3,347	77	29,759	942
1905–06	14,312	86	5,592	305	4,893	1,088	6,545	454	1,974	55	33,316	1,988
1910–11	17,292	150	6,096	453	6,237	2,149	9,933	1,148	1,632	54	41,190	3,954
1915–16	3,503	130	2,727	735	2,417	1,412	3,263	765	656	166	12,566	3,208
1920–21	17,376	861	10,918	1,326	7,892	3,182	11,366	1,417	2,197	511	49,727	7,297
1925–26	17,415	1,507	12,596	1,638	12,244	5,750	12,286	2,158	3,701	1,179	58,242	12,232
1930–31	20,871	2,576	15,495	3,110	18,386	9,106	18,086	3,387	5,486	2,009	78,324	20,188
1935–36	21,568	3,131	11,329	2,578	17,221	8,247	17,699	3,829	5,654	2,490	73,471	20,275
1940–41a	21,541	4,385	15,158	4,308	19,702	10,650	13,691	3,230	6,293	3,324	76,385	25,897
1945–46	40,553	9,318	21,947	5,853	27,778	15,021	19,586	4,172	8,051	4,261	117,915	38,625
1950–51	36,888	9,669	26,156	6,489	35,156	19,232	29,083	6,508	6,810	3,713	134,093	45,611
1955–56	35,486	10,113	38,290	10,525	41,785	23,877	29,091	6,660	7,594	4,199	152,246	55,374
1960–61	33,634	9,792	68,062	21,928	63,395	38,962	30,587	7,724	8,697	5,162	203,375	83,568
1961–62	38,469	11,275	75,282	24,196	73,376	46,490	36,203	9,289	9,300	5,564	232,610	96,814
1962–63	45,511	12,939	88,175	*	85,063	*	37,633	10,194	10,174	6,081	266,556	*

*Not available.
a. Until 1940–41 inclusive, the numbers include students at the University of Algiers.

significant impact on living standards until after 1950 (see fig. 1.2).

Table 1.4, showing the relative shares of the various faculties, highlights a reversal which emerges less clearly from the absolute figures (which show a rise for all disciplines). Arts and Science students now account for 65 percent of the student population, whereas they represented only about 25 percent at the beginning of the century. Over the same period, the Law and Medicine faculties evolved in a symmetrically opposite way; Pharmacy declined slightly (see fig. 1.3).

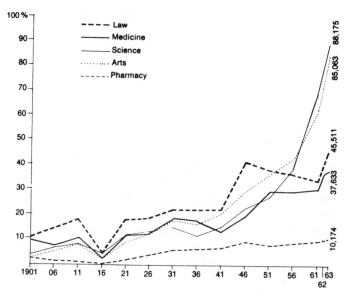

Fig. 1.2 Number of Students in Each Discipline (by thousands)

Beyond the short-term fluctuations, it can be seen that the structure of the student milieu has radically changed in the course of half a century, as shown by fig. 1.4.

The figures in table 1.5 retrace the stages in a major cultural transformation, in which the proportion of female students has risen in half a century from 3 percent to 41 percent.[3] But this growth has varied from one discipline to another.

The disciplines did not include female students equally early, equally quickly, or equally steadily. Female students first made

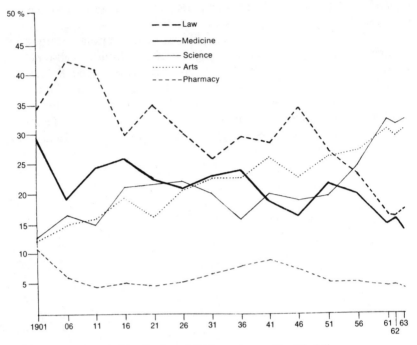

Fig. 1.3 Distribution of Students Among the Disciplines

their entry into the Arts faculties; the proportion of women there was already 34 percent by 1911, whereas elsewhere it was below 15 percent. Women appeared latest in the Law faculties; in 1931 only 12 percent of Law students were women. In Science, unlike Arts or Pharmacy, there has been a regular increase, greater than that in Law and Medicine.

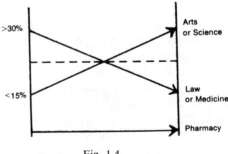

Fig. 1.4

Medicine and Pharmacy have to be considered separately from the other disciplines. Pharmacy started to attract female students in 1911, at a speed which by 1941 had brought it up to the level of Arts (more than half the students in each of these disciplines

TABLE 1.4 Distribution of Students among the Disciplines (in relative values)

Years	Distribution Per 100 Students					
	Law	Science	Arts	Medicine	Pharmacy	Total
1900–01	33.9	13.2	12.6	28.9	11.4	100
1905–06	42.9	16.8	14.7	19.6	6	100
1910–11	41.8	14.8	15.2	24.1	4.1	100
1915–16	27.9	21.7	19.2	26	5.2	100
1920–21	34.9	21.9	15.9	22.8	4.5	100
1925–26	29.9	21.6	21	21.1	6.4	100
1930–31	26.6	19.8	23.5	23.1	7	100
1935–36	29.4	15.4	23.4	24.1	7.7	100
1940–41	28.2	19.9	25.8	17.9	8.2	100
1945–46	34.4	18.6	23.6	16.6	6.8	100
1950–51	27.5	19.5	26.2	21.7	5.1	100
1955–56	23.3	25.2	27.5	19.2	5.0	100
1960–61	16.5	33.5	30.7	15	4.3	100
1961–62	16.5	32.4	31.5	15.6	4.0	100
1962–63	17.1	33.1	31.9	14.1	3.8	100

TABLE 1.5. Percentage of Female Students in Each Discipline

	Law	Science	Arts	Medi-cine	Phar-macy	All Disci-plines
1900–01	0.1	2.5	6.5	5.9	2.3	3.2
1905–06	0.6	5.4	22.2	6.9	2.8	6.0
1910–11	0.9	7.4	34.4	11.5	3.3	9.6
1915–16	3.7	26.9	58.4	23.4	25.3	25.5
1920–21	4.9	12.1	40.3	12.5	23.2	14.7
1925–26	8.6	13.0	47.0	17.6	31.8	21.0
1930–31	12.3	20.0	49.5	18.7	36.6	25.8
1935–36	14.5	22.7	47.9	21.6	44.0	27.6
1940–41	20.3	28.4	54.0	23.6	52.8	33.9
1945–46	22.3	26.7	54.1	21.3	53.0	32.7
1950–51	26.2	24.8	54.7	22.4	54.5	34.0
1955–56	28.5	27.5	57.1	22.9	55.3	36.4
1960–61	29.1	32.2	62.4	25.2	59.3	41.1
1961–62	29.3	32.1	63.3	25.6	59.8	41.6

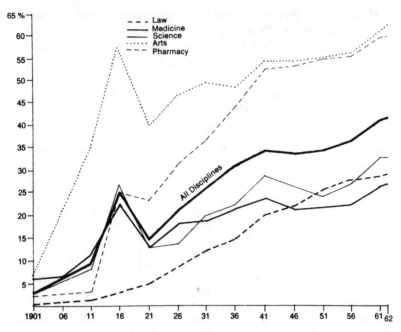

Fig. 1.5 Percentage of Female Students in Each Discipline

then being women). As for Medicine, which is now the discipline with the fewest female students—from 1901 to 1911, it had a higher proportion of female students than Science, Law, or Pharmacy, but the subsequent growth rate has remained low.

Earlier or later take-off, slower or faster growth, more or less regularity, and the rough correspondence between early take-off and rapid growth[4] are probably explained by the fact that the different subjects and the different careers to which they lead are differently qualified with respect to the models and norms which define the standard image of female activity. Each discipline can be considered from two standpoints—in terms of the opposition between "artists" and "scientists" and in terms of the occupation it prepares for. Arts subjects combine all the advantages, since they train for the job most generally conceded to women, that is, teaching, and coincide with the widely held notion of the "naturally" feminine gifts.

Among the professions that were traditionally the preserve of the bourgeoisie, only Pharmacy has seen a strong rise in the number of female students. In Medicine, where until 1911 there was a higher proportion of female students than in other disciplines, this tendency was not sustained. This may be because, on the one hand, there was a switch to Pharmacy on the part of female students of bourgeois origin (as evidenced by the distribution by social origin, which shows Medicine and Pharmacy to be the most bourgeois faculties) and, on the other hand, rational or ethical resistances may have held back female enrollment by reducing, here more than elsewhere, the proportion of women in the recruitment from other social classes.

1.6. *Higher Education Enrollment Rates, 1911–63*[5]

Between 1911 and 1962 the number of students in higher education increased sixfold and the rate of enrollment increased sevenfold.[6] At present (1963), increased access is the sole cause of the growth in numbers, since the children born after 1945 (when the birth rate started to rise again) have not yet reached higher education.[7]

TABLE 1.6.

Year	French Population (age 19–24)	Student Population (age 19–24)	Rate of Enrollment %	
1911	3,707,000	25,940	0.7	
1936	3,285,000	46,488	1.4	over the
1946	3,760,000	76,810	2.0	half-century
1954	3,770,462	92,341	2.4	
1957	3,650,000	104,330	2.8	
1958	3,613,144	118,295	3.3	
1959	3,591,047	126,021	3.5	
1960	3,509,000	126,596	3.6	over six years
1961	3,409,171	129,535	3.8	
1962	3,383,600	148,699	4.4	
1963	3,420,700	172,611	5.0	

French Students' Social Origins

We have used three sets of statistics on students' social origins. This leads to some redundancy, but these different approaches to the same phenomenon are needed in order to bring out the various aspects of inequality in relation to education.

The first type of statistics (tables 1.7 and 1.8) show the proportion of students from the various social classes in the whole

TABLE 1.7 Number of Students in Each Discipline (academic year 1961–62)

Occupational Categories	Law			Science			Arts	
	M	F	Both	M	F	Both	M	F
Farm workers	107	39	146	314	140	454	232	313
Farmers	1,234	608	1,842	3,112	1,395	4,507	1,586	2,229
Domestic servants	183	77	260	581	230	811	231	331
Industrial workers	1,125	540	1,665	4,353	1,743	6,096	1,939	2,765
Clerical workers	2,216	1,044	3,260	4,419	2,079	6,498	1,414	2,566
Industrial and commercial proprietors	3,904	1,908	5,812	8,172	3,787	11,959	4,233	8,141
of which: Industrialists	965	458	1,423	1,245	537	1,782	1,102	2,352
Lower-rank executives	3,926	1,657	5,583	7,638	4,257	11,895	5,053	10,027
Professions, senior executives	6,291	3,041	9,332	12,290	7,189	19,479	4,971	11,420
Private income, no occupation	2,464	984	3,448	3,860	1,681	5,541	1,641	2,348
Other	2,157	1,017	3,174	2,383	1,187	3,570	1,660	2,364
General total	23,607	10,915	34,522	47,122	23,688	70,810	22,950	42,504

TABLE 1.8 Breakdown by Discipline and Sex (academic year 1961–62)

Occupational Categories	Law			Science			Arts	
	M	F	Both	M	F	Both	M	F
Farm workers	0.45	0.35	0.4	0.7	0.6	0.6	1.0	0.7
Farmers	5.2	5.6	5.3	6.6	5.9	6.3	6.9	5.2
Domestic servants	0.8	0.7	0.8	1.2	1	1.1	1.0	0.8
Industrial workers	4.8	4.9	4.8	9.2	7.3	8.6	8.4	6.5
Clerical workers	9.4	9.5	9.4	9.4	8.8	9.1	6.2	6.0
Industrial and commercial proprietors	16.5	17.5	16.8	17.3	16	16.9	18.4	19.2
of which: Industrialists	4.1	4.2	4.1	2.6	2.3	2.5	4.8	5.5
Lower-rank executives	16.65	15.2	16.2	16.2	18	16.9	22.0	23.6
Professions, senior executives	26.65	27.85	27.1	26.1	30.3	27.6	21.7	26.9
Private income, no occupation	10.4	9.1	10.0	8.2	7.1	7.8	7.2	5.5
Other	9.15	9.3	9.2	5.1	5.0	5.1	7.2	5.6
Total %	100	100	100	100	100	100	100	100
Total number of students	23,607	10,915	34,522	47,122	23,688	70,810	22,950	42,504

Both	Medicine			Pharmacy			Totals		General Total
	M	F	Both	M	F	Both	M	F	Both
545	39	12	51	5	7	12	697	511	1,208
3,815	941	251	1,192	162	273	435	7,035	4,756	11,791
562	136	67	203	9	9	18	1,140	714	1,854
4,704	750	258	1,008	63	125	188	8,230	5,431	13,661
3,980	1,728	757	2,485	176	270	446	9,953	6,716	16,669
12,364	3,962	1,469	5,431	776	1,193	1,969	21,037	16,498	37,535
3,454	871	442	1,313	171	277	448	4,354	4,066	8,420
15,080	3,008	1,151	4,159	463	741	1,204	20,088	17,833	37,921
16,391	8,042	3,239	11,281	1,481	2,410	3,891	33,075	27,229	60,374
3,989	1,075	348	1,423	164	204	368	9,204	5,565	14,769
4,024	3,701	1,378	5,079	114	136	250	10,015	6,082	16,097
65,454	23,382	8,930	32,312	3,413	5,368	8,781	120,474	91,405	211,879

Both	Medicine			Pharmacy			All Disciplines		
	M	F	Both	M	F	Both	M	F	Both
0.8	0.2	0.1	0.2	0.1	0.1	0.1	0.6	0.6	0.6
5.9	4.0	2.8	3.7	4.8	5.1	5.0	5.8	5.2	5.6
0.9	0.6	0.7	0.6	0.3	0.2	0.2	1.0	0.8	0.9
7.2	3.2	2.9	3.1	1.8	2.35	2.2	6.8	5.9	6.4
6.0	7.4	8.5	7.7	5.8	5.0	5.0	8.3	7.3	7.9
18.9	16.9	16.5	16.8	22.7	22.25	22.5	17.4	18.0	17.7
5.3	3.7	4.9	4.1	5.0	5.2	5.1	3.6	4.4	4.0
23.0	12.9	12.9	12.9	13.6	13.8	13.7	16.7	19.5	17.8
25.1	34.3	36.3	34.9	43.4	44.9	44.2	27.5	29.9	28.5
6.1	4.6	3.9	4.4	4.8	3.8	4.2	7.6	6.1	7.0
6.1	15.8	15.4	15.7	3.3	2.5	2.9	8.3	6.7	7.6
100	100	100	100	100	100	100	100	100	100
65,454	23,382	8,930	32,312	3,413	5,368	8,781	120,474	91,405	211,879

TABLE 1.9   Number of Students per 1000 Economically Active Persons Classified by Occupational Category

Occupational Category	Breakdown of Students (1961–62)		Working Population (1962 census)		Number of students per 1,000 active persons in category of origin
	Number	Per 1,000	Number	Per 1,000	
Farm workers	1,208	6	829,600	43	1.4
Farmers	11,791	56	3,011,600	157	1.4
Domestic servants	1,834	9	1,042,020	54	1.7
Industrial workers	13,661	64	7,024,040	367	1.9
Clerical workers	16,669	79	2,416,300	126	6.8
Industrial and commercial proprietors	37,535	177	1,996,560	104	18
Industrialists	8,420	40	78,780	4	106.8
Artisans	1,376	39	611,000	32	13.7
Shopkeepers	20,739	98	1,287,340	66	16.1
Fishing-boat owners	—	—	19,440	7	
Lower managerial	37,921	178	1,490,500	78	25.4
Professions and senior managerial	60,374	91	761,040	40	79.3
Liberal professions	20,900	168	124,340	6	168
Teachers	11,464	285	126,040	7	91
Senior administrative executives	28,010	55	510,660	27	55
Private income, no occupation	14,769	70			11
Other	16,097	76	592,800	31	
Total	211,879	1,000	19,164,460	1,000	11

student population and in each discipline. These are the figures most commonly used to describe the unequal representation of the various strata of French society in higher education. It can be seen that if, to the 28.5 percent of students whose fathers are senior executives or professionals, one adds the 4 percent whose fathers are industrialists, then the group we have characterized as culturally privileged accounted for 30 percent of the university population in 1962.

But these figures give only a very incomplete picture of educational privilege, since the social categories least represented in higher education are at the same time those most numerous in the working population. The statistical chances of university entrance are often assessed in terms of the ratio of the number of students from a given socio-occupational category to the number of economically active persons in that category. We give this second type of statistics here, although they enable only a fairly rough estimate of objective opportunities (table 1.9). But, by allowing a separate count to be made of the children of industrialists and professionals, they demonstrate that it is in this group that the chances of university entrance are greatest.

The third type of statistics, aiming to give a more precise estimation of educational opportunity, have been used in the text (page 3). Their methodological justification will be found below.

Evaluating Educational Opportunity

The table on page 3 presents two sorts of probabilities. The first column gives the *objective probability* which a child of given sex, whose father has a given occupation, has of *normally* entering higher education. It is provided by the ratio:

$$\frac{\text{students enrolled for first time, from a given social category}}{\text{cohort of children from same social category}}$$

The following columns indicate the chances that a (male or female) student from a given social category, enrolling at university for the first time, has of taking this or that course. These are conditional probabilities which presuppose entry into higher education. They are expressed in the ratio:

$$\frac{\begin{array}{c}\text{students enrolled for first time in a given discipline, from}\\ \text{a given social category}\end{array}}{\begin{array}{c}\text{students from same social category enrolled for first time}\\ \text{at university}\end{array}}$$

To avoid giving a disproportionate (and, in this case, meaningless) weight to the longest courses (for example, medicine) we have chosen to base this calculation of chances on the intake into each discipline.

Methodological Note[8]

On the basis of the figure supplied by the BUS for the academic year 1961–62 (breakdown of faculty students by parents' socio-occupational category), the object is to establish the *objective probability* a child has (say, at birth) of normally entering higher education, the father's occupation being known.

The birth records of the age groups a certain number of whose members entered university in 1961 would (with a few reservations) provide an answer to the problem, since they indicate the father's occupation at the time of the child's birth and would therefore show the distribution of live births by socio-occupational category.

Statements of occupation are usually vague, and this always creates difficulties, but much more serious are the systematic biases inspired by the search for flattering titles. Studies now in progress at the Ministry of Education indicate that lycée pupils' statements about their parents' occupation should be treated with considerable skepticism.

In a society in which the social structure was stationary and behavior patterns were sufficiently stable over time, the A ratios as defined below would indeed correspond to the objective probability we are looking for:

$$A = \frac{\text{new students from a cohort[8]}}{\text{cohort of children from a given social category}}$$

They are different from B ratios:

$$B = \frac{\text{new students from a given social category}}{\text{cohort of children from this social category (at same age)}}$$

B ratios refer to university enrollment, A ratios to birth.

If social behaviors are stable over time, the operational ratio, for the individual concerned, is likely to lie between A and B.

B^1 ratios can be written thus:

$$B^1 = B^1_1 + B^1_2 + \ldots \ldots + B^1_k$$

B^1 is the proportion originating from social category k, so that the number of students who belonged, at birth, to social category k is:

$$N^1 B^1_k + N^2 B^2_k + \ldots \ldots + N^k B^k_k$$

(N represents the corresponding numbers in the cohort).

Dividing by M^k (numbers in the cohorts at birth) we get:

$$A^k = \frac{N^i}{M^k} B^1_k + \ldots \ldots + \frac{N^k}{M^k} B^k_k$$

where N^i/M^k is the mathematical likelihood of moving from k to i, for a man belonging to category k at the age when he can be a father.

To the extent that changes in social category could no longer take place after that age, we would, of course, get:

$$\frac{M^k}{N^k} = 1 \text{ and } \frac{N^i}{N^k} (i \neq k) = 0$$

and:

$$A^k = B^k_{\;k} = B^k \text{ (or } A = B)$$

In approximate terms, this is true of categories to which entry is dependent on:

possession of economic capital (industrialists, shopkeepers)
possession of a university qualification (senior executives)

But for categories where there is not the same entry restriction, the situation is different, and $A \neq B$. Since it can only be a question of estimating orders of magnitude, the two concepts can be regarded as equivalent.

In fact, we know B^k and, at best, we can envisage estimating N^i/M^k; in any case, the A system cannot be completely resolved in general (a system of n equations with n^2 unknown quantities).

The B ratios would appear to be of greater operational value than the A ratios; they are sufficient to determine subjective expectations for the period which concerns us (that is, the probability of entering higher education as the agents might spontaneously assess it).

Therefore, it is only possible to estimate B, and only very imperfectly.

A. To estimate the distribution of the live births during an average year between 1941 and 1943 (from which come most of the *new* students in the academic year 1961–62) by parents' social category, we shall use:

an estimate of the number of married women of child-bearing age in each social category;

an indicator of the differential fertility by social category, namely, the distribution of the *male* active population, married and under age 50 (of which a proportion that is probably independent of social category have wives under age 45), corrected by an indicator of differential fertility. In other words, we shall calculate the products: $H^{50}xf$

H^{50} is the number of married active men aged under 50.

f is the mean number of children per family. $HfM/\Sigma Hf$ is the number in a cohort of children from the corresponding social category.

Lacking the necessary data, we are unable to take account of differential death rate, so that in place of B we, in fact, have a slightly lower ratio which is liable to result in a slight distortion in the differential analysis. In a more precise calculation, we would have calculated the terms

$$\frac{HfS^{19}_0M}{\Sigma Hf}$$

Where S^{19}_0 is the mean survival rate at age 19.

B. The BUS data also only allow an approximate calculation, since:

Social category of origin is given for the whole student population and not for first-year students alone, so that those taking very long courses (for example, medicine) are relatively overrepresented. We have had to assume that the distribution by social origin of newly enrolled students was the same as the distribution for the student population as a whole.

Distribution by sex is not given for all students. Here, too, it was assumed that, within each discipline, this distribution was the same for the new intake and for the whole student group. This hypothesis is fairly accurate: the estimates provided by the BUS (distribution by sex of students enrolled for first time in 1963–64) show that there are proportionately slightly more girls in the first than in subsequent years, but this difference remains very small.

Two categories that are relatively numerous, "Private income" and "Others," present special difficulties.

2.Selected Documents and Survey Findings[1]

Social Origin and Student Life (Tables 2.1–2.5)
2.1 and 2.2 *Source of Income*
It can be seen from tables 2.1 and 2.2 that the proportion of students whose resources are derived from a scholarship or a part-time job (as opposed to those supported by their families) varies with social origin, but the link appears to be stronger among the "philosophers" than among the "sociologists."

2.3 *Accommodation*
Table 2.3 shows that the higher a student's social origin, the more likely he is to live in his parents' home, which implies a particular type of experience of daily life and work. More fully accepted or more strongly felt dependence gives rise to quite specific conducts, attitudes, and opinions among students who live at home.

2.4 and 2.5 *Part-time Jobs while Studying*
The proportion of students who have to take jobs while studying declines steadily as social origin rises. But, as is shown by comparison of sociology students with philosophy students, this proportion appears to be lower, whatever the social origin, when the discipline is more "traditional."

Social Origin and Academic Behavior and Attitudes[2]
(Tables 2.6–2.13)
A discipline like sociology, which can enter into various combinations of subjects studied simultaneously, reveals that academic "dilettantism" is particularly characteristic of upper-class students. In the sociology student group, the proportion of students enrolled

119

TABLE 2.1 Source of Income: Philosophy Students

Father's Occupation	Source of Income						
	Scholarship %	Family Support %	Job %	Scholarship + Family %	Job + Family %	Total %	Number of Students
Agricultural, industrial workers, clerical workers, junior supervisory	27	14.5	21	21	16.5	100	(48)
Artisans, shopkeepers	22	22	11	6	39	100	(18)
Lower managerial	12.5	37.5	12.5	15	22.5	100	(40)
Senior managerial, professions	11.5	58	1.5	11	18	100	(71)
Number of Students	(30)	(67)	(18)	(25)	(37)		(177)

TABLE 2.2 Source of Income: Sociology Students

Father's Occupation	Source of Income						
	Scholarship %	Family Support %	Job %	Scholarship + Family %	Job + Family %	Total %	Number of Students
Agricultural, industrial workers, clerical workers, junior supervisory	23	10	43.5	13.5	10	100	(30)
Artisans, shopkeepers	15	45	20	7.5	12.5	100	(40)
Lower managerial	15	39	22	15	9	100	(46)
Senior managerial, professions	13.5	50	10	7	19.5	100	(98)
Number of Students	(33)	(88)	(41)	(21)	(31)		(214)

TABLE 2.3.   Accommodations: Philosophy and Sociology Students

Father's Occupation	Parents' home %	University residence %	Private lodgings %	Total %	Number of Students
Type of Accommodation					
Agricultural, industrial workers, clerical workers, junior supervisory	29.5	56	14.5	100	(95)
Artisans, shopkeepers	34	57	9	100	(65)
Lower managerial	35	53	12	100	(91)
Senior managerial, professions	50	37	13	100	(189)
Number of Students	(177)	(208)	(55)		(440)

TABLE 2.4.   Part-time Jobs While Studying: Philosophy Students

	Job %	No Job %	Total %
Agricultural, industrial workers, clerical workers, junior supervisory	36	64	100
Artisans, shopkeepers	25	75	100
Lower management	25	75	100
Senior managerial, professions	11	89	100

TABLE 2.5.   Part-time Jobs While Studying: Sociology Students

	Job %	No Job %	Total %
Agricultural, industrial workers, clerical workers, junior supervisory	53.5	46.5	100
Artisans, shopkeepers	28	72	100
Lower managerial	24.5	75.5	100
Senior managerial, professions	25.5	74.5	100

TABLE 2.6. Academic Options—Section Taken in Baccalauréat Part 1: Philosophy and Sociology Students

Father's Occupation	Baccalauréat Course					
	Exemption %	Latin-Greek %	Latin-Modern Langs. %	Latin-Science %	Modern or Technical %	Total %
Agricultural, industrial workers	6.8	20.5	16	4.2	52	100
Clerical, junior supervisory		20	33	6	41	100
Artisans, shopkeepers	1.5	12.5	48.5	7.8	29.5	100
Lower managerial		24	35	13	28	100
Senior managerial, professions		26	41	17	17	100

in courses in several subjects in the same year rises with social origin (see table 2.7).[3]

When sociology students are asked whether they would rather study their own society or Third World countries and anthropology, "exotic" choices are more frequent as social origin rises (see table 2.8).

In the sociology student group, as in the female student group, the level of union membership is much higher among students

TABLE 2.7. Multiple Courses: Sociology Students

Father's Occupation	No %	Yes %	Total %
Agricultural, industrial workers, clerical, junior supervisory	56	44	100
Artisans, shopkeepers	45	55	100
Lower managerial	42	58	100
Senior managerial, professions	32	68	100

TABLE 2.8. Preferred Object of Study: Sociology Students

Father's Occupation	Europe %	Third World or Anthropology %	Total %
Agricultural, industrial workers, clerical, junior supervisory	44	56	100
Artisans, shopkeepers, lower managerial	42	58	100
Senior managerial, professions	26.5	73.5	100

TABLE 2.9. Involvement in Student Union: All-Female Sample

Father's Occupation	Member %	Indifferent or Hostile %	Total %
Agricultural, industrial workers	70.7	29.3	100
Junior supervisory, artisans, shopkeepers	60.8	39.2	100
Lower managerial	60.6	39.4	100
Senior management, professions	53.1	46.9	100

TABLE 2.10. Involvement in Student Union: Sociology Students

Father's Occupation	Official %	Member %	Indifferent or Hostile %	Total %
Agricultural, industrial workers, clerical, junior supervisory	18	71	11	100
Artisans, shopkeepers, lower managerial, senior managerial, professions	16	50	34	100

from the lower classes (tables 2.9 and 2.10). But the difference seems to disappear when it comes to union *responsibility*. Here the upper- and middle-class students have a presence which does not correspond to their lower level of unionization.

2.11. *Scholastic Age and Social Origin*

From faculty entrance onward, the histogram in figure 2.1 representing the age distribution of students from the different social classes shows that the proportion of students who are at the modal scholastic age (relative to the whole group of students from that social class) is higher in the more privileged categories; or (which amounts to the same thing) that the distribution is more regular the higher the social origin (see table 2.11). The age distribution for lower-class students is even slightly bimodal. As one moves through the university *cursus,* the distributions diverge more and more in their appearance, with the minimum age ceasing to be represented sooner in the case of the lower classes. In the final years, there is also an upward tendency in the proportion of students from the lower classes. This reveals another disadvantage suffered by these students—stagnation in their educational careers (repeats and resits), which, by forcing them to stay longer at university, gives them relatively greater weight in the overall statistics of social origin and partly disguises the elimination of which they are the victims. The type of stagnation characteristic of upper-class students (an increasing spread of these students' modal age) can be explained by the same argument that applies to students' representation in the "refuge" disciplines (see pp. 7–8).

The average number of persons known rises steadily with social origin (see table 2.12). The increase in mutual acquaintance ac-

TABLE 2.11. Age Distribution

	Mode		Median		Mean		Typical Deviation	
Father's Occupation	1st Year	2d Year	1st Year	2d Year	1st Year	2d Year	1st Year	2d Year
Working classes	19	20	20	21	20–5*	21–8	1.88	2.1
Lower-middle classes	19	20	19	21	19–10	21–1	1.72	1.69
Upper classes	19	21	19	20	19–7	20–10	1.48	1.58
All	19	20	19	21	20	21–2	1.72	1.74

*20–5: read 20 years 5 months.

TABLE 2.12. Levels of Mutual Acquaintance
(average number of fellow-students known per student
in each social category)

	Degree of Acquaintance		
Father's Occupation	A	A or C	A or C or N or S
Agricultural, industrial workers	2.2	6.5	14.4
Clerical	2.8	8.5	18
Lower managerial	3	7.1	15
Industrial proprietors, shopkeepers	4	9.1	21
Senior managerial, professions	4.3	9.6	19
All	3.2	8.4	19

A: through a regular common activity
C: at least one conversation
N: known only by name
S: known only by sight

cording to social origin is more marked in the case of closer types
of acquaintance: 14 to 19 when persons known by any means at
all are counted, 6 to 9 when conversation is the measure of acquaintance, and 2 to 4 when only persons known through a common activity are counted (criterion of close acquaintance).

Whatever type of acquaintance is considered, the average number of fellow students known declines systematically as one moves
from the front rows to the back of the lecture theater (see table
2.13). Ease or self-assurance within the university system, roughly

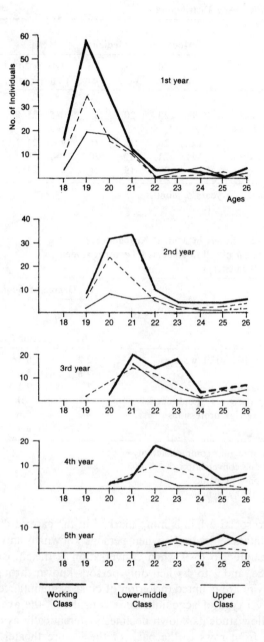

Fig. 2.1

TABLE 2.13. Variation in Mutual Acquaintance by Position in Amphitheater
(average number of fellow students known per student)

		Degree of Acquaintance	
Position	A	A or C	A or C or N or S
Front third	5.1	9.7	23
Middle third	3.4	8.6	17
Rear third	2.3	7.1	15
All	3.2	8.4	19

A: through a regular common activity
C: at least one conversation
N: known only by name
S: known only by sight

measured by position in the hall, is, thus, not unrelated to the sociability techniques characteristic of the cultured classes.

Social Origin and Knowledge of the Theater (Tables 2.14–2.18)
2.14 and 2.15 *Variation in Knowledge of Theater by Father's Occupational Category and Type of Access to Plays*

In table 2.14, simple comparison of the medians shows that the number of plays seen in live performance rises as one moves from the lower classes to the middle and upper classes. In all cases, the modal figure is between 4 and 8, but a fraction (25%) of the children of senior executives have scores higher than the mode for their category and the mode of the survey group as a whole. There are no significant differences in access to plays through radio and television; for all categories, reading is the most frequent means of access to plays.

The results correspond to a hierarchy by social origin in the case of acquaintance through stage performances (see table 2.15). Given that in the case of direct access to the theater, the cleavage is between the children of senior executives and all other students, we regrouped the students in these categories, finding that the difference in scores is statistically very significant: $X^2 = 31.27$, significant at P.01.

Knowledge of the most consecrated types of art (especially those consecrated by the educational system) is the most strongly represented, whatever the social origin (see table 2.16).

TABLE 2.14. Knowledge of Theater: Degree Students

Father's Occupation	Number of Plays Seen on Stage						Median
	0	1–3	4–8	9–14	15–18	Total	
Agricultural, industrial workers	5	8	11			24	1–3
Clerical, junior supervisory	9	21	24	2		56	1–3
Artisans, shopkeepers	4	16	17	4		41	4–8
Lower managerial	7	21	23	7		58	4–8
Senior managerial	9	21	58	25	3	116	4–8
Subtotal	34	87	133	38	3	295	4–8
No reply	1	8	7	3		19	
Total	35	95	140	41	3	314	4–8

Father's Occupation	Number of Plays on Radio or Television						Median
	0	1–3	4–8	9–14	15–18	Total	
Agricultural, industrial workers	9	10	5			24	1–3
Clerical, junior supervisory	14	22	12	8		56	1–3
Artisans, shopkeepers	12	18	9	2		41	1–3
Lower managerial	13	22	20	3		58	1–3
Senior managerial	40	38	33	5		116	1–3
Subtotal	88	110	79	18		295	1–3
No reply	6	8	5			19	
Total	94	118	84	18		314	1–3

Father's Occupation	Number of Plays Read						Median
	0	1–3	4–8	9–14	15–18	Total	
Agricultural, industrial workers	1	2	7	13	1	24	9–14
Clerical, junior supervisory	2	1	28	22	3	56	4–8
Artisans, shopkeepers		5	19	14	3	41	4–8
Lower managerial	1	3	23	29	2	58	9–14
Senior managerial	3	6	48	54	5	116	9–14
Subtotal	7	17	125	132	14	295	4–8
No reply			11	8		19	
Total	7	17	136	140	14	314	4–8

TABLE 2.15. Whole Sample

Father's Occupation	Plays Seen on Stage			Radio, T. V.			Plays Read		
	less than 3 dramatists %	more than 3 %	Number of students	less than 3 %	more than 3 %	Number of students	less than 9 %	more than 9 %	Number of students
Agricultural	66	34	42	78	22	42	54	46	42
Industrial workers	82	18	29	41	59	29	68	32	29
Clerical, junior supervisory	66	34	144	55	45	144	59	41	144
Artisans, shopkeepers	62	38	98	63	37	98	61	39	98
Lower managerial	58	42	117	56	44	117	50	50	117
Senior managerial	39	61	251	59	41	251	52	48	251
Total number of students	374	307	681	404	277	681	378	303	681

TABLE 2.16. Knowledge of the Different Types of Theater, by Social Origin: Degree Students

Father's Occupation	A		B		C		D		
	Number	High Score %	Number	High Score %	Number	High Score %	Number	High Score %	Total
Agricultural, industrial workers	22	92	20	83	8	30	13	54	24
Clerical, junior supervisory, artisans, shopkeepers, lower managerial	148	94	137	88	88	57	89	57	155
Senior managerial	111	96	106	91	84	72	78	67	116

A: *Classics* (Hugo, Marivaux, Shakespeare, Sophocles)
B: *Consecrated moderns* (Camus, Claudel, Ibsen, Montherlant, Sartre)
C: *Avant-garde* (Beckett, Brecht, Ionesco, Pirandello)
D: *Middlebrow* ("*théâtre de boulevard*": Achard, Aymé, Feydeau, Roussin)

But the structure of the different sorts of knowledge varies with social origin. For the lower classes (the children of agricultural and industrial workers), there are marked differences between tastes for the types of art most consecrated academically (classics and consecrated moderns) and artistic interests less tied to schooling; as social origin rises, this disparity is reduced and is lowest among the children of senior executives.

The meaning of these shifts in patterns of knowledge is clear. Given that working-class and lower-middle-class students are restricted to a mediated access mainly organized by the school system (reading), it is natural that their choices should fix on the most "scholastic" works; this tendency could only be reinforced by the attitude to schooling and culture which they owe to their background.

The disparity according to social origin is greatest in the case of avant-garde theater, where there is a very significant difference statistically between the three class groups. ($X^2 = 15$, significant at P.01.)

It can be seen from table 2.17 how strongly social background can influence students' cultural behavior. Not only is the average number of plays seen in live performance consistently higher when the father's or grandfather's social category is higher, or when both are simultaneously higher, but also, for a given value of each of these variables, the other tends, in its own right, to cause a hierarchical ordering of the scores. In other words, with grandfathers of equivalent backgrounds, the scores tend to be higher when the father's position is higher, and, with fathers of equivalent backgrounds, the grandfather's position also tends to cause a hierarchical ordering of the scores.

The same tendencies are still apparent, but much less clearly, in the case of reading, which, in the absence of direct contact, can fulfill a compensatory role (see table 2.18).

Social Origin and Knowledge of Music (Tables 2.19 and 2.20)

In table 2.19, simple comparison of the medians shows that the number of works heard at concerts rises as one moves from the working classes and the petite bourgeoisie to the children of senior executives. Comparison of the medians indicates that direct access through concerts is rarer than indirect access through records. On the other hand, among the children of senior executives, the dis-

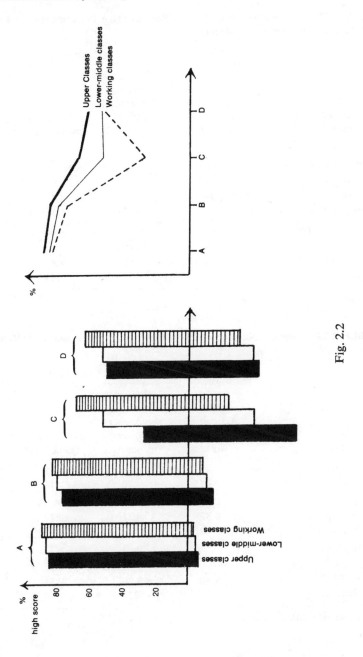

Fig. 2.2

TABLE 2.17. Average Number of Plays Seen in Stage Performance, by Father's and Grandfather's Occupational Category

Grandfather's Occupation	Father's Occupation			
	Agriculture, Industrial workers	Clerical, artisans, shopkeepers, lower managerial	Senior managerial	Average by grandfather's category
Agricultural, industrial workers	3.00 45*	3 70	4.37 16	3.16 131
Clerical, artisans, shopkeepers, lower managerial	1.75 10	3.57 127	4.43 51	3.73 188
Senior managerial	0	5.00 30	4.86 97	4.68 127
Average by father's category	2.74 55	3.58 227	4.68 164	446

*Number of students in category.

TABLE 2.18. Average Number of Plays Read, by Father's and Grandfather's Occupational Category

Grandfather's Occupation	Father's Occupation			
	Agriculture, industrial workers	Clerical, artisans, shopkeepers, lower managerial	Senior managerial	Average by grandfather's category
Agricultural, industrial workers	7.93 45*	7.75 70	9.12 16	7.98 131
Clerical, artisans, shopkeepers, lower managerial	8.87 10	8.21 127	8.37 51	8.28 188
Senior managerial	0	9.23 30	8.55 97	8.83 127
Average by father's category	8.38 55	8.20 227	8.55 164	446

*Number of students in category.

tribution of concert-hall acquaintance is distinctly bimodal: class "0" and class "4 to 10" (with one third of the individuals in this social category having a score equal or superior to the highest mode). We find here a characteristic tendency of the category of senior executives' children: a considerable fraction of this category (a third or a quarter) set themselves apart from the rest of the category as well as from the whole student population. This seems to indicate that the cultural privileges attached to high social origin do not operate in all cases.

The classics beat the moderns overall, with the only composers who really achieve a consensus (who are mentioned more than 500 times) being Mozart (627), Beethoven (626), Bach (593), and Brahms (538) (see table 2.20). Certain names seem to be linked to class cultural habits, since they are cited with significantly greater frequency according to social origin. This is the case with: Stravinsky ($X^2 = 17.2$), Debussy ($X^2 = 17.7$).

The Influence of Age (Tables 2.21–2.28)

In a number of cases, we find age-related variations running in opposite directions among sociology and philosophy students. Whereas among philosophy students, religious affiliation increases as one moves from the younger to the older students, it decreases among the sociologists; conversely, extreme left-wing political opinions decline among the former and increase among the latter. To account for these apparent oddities, it has to be borne in mind, first, that in contrast to the philosophy degree, a teaching qualification, sociology is a discipline with relatively uncertain career outlets; it is, therefore, a refuge for students who have often come from more classical disciplines. Secondly, if one remembers that above-average age in a student is a sign of failure or a lack of adaptation to the university, it may be concluded that seniority within this group represents the tendential reality of this group, or even its pathology. Finally, given that a number of indices suggest that sociology students hold more strongly than others to the values of the intelligentsia, it is not surprising that the oldest of the sociologists should present the most accentuated form of the "intellectual" type.

It can be seen that, in student union activity as in political activity, the difference between male and female students, which

TABLE 2.19.   Variation in Knowledge of Music by Father's Occupational Category and Type of Access to Works: Degree Students and Students in Propédeutique[4]

Father's Occupation	Concerts				Radio, T. V.	
	0	1–3	4–10	Median	0	1–3
Agricultural, industrial workers	45	12	14	0	9	13
Clerical, junior supervisory	73	40	31	0	22	21
Artisans, shopkeepers, lower managerial	98	66	51	1–3	35	46
Senior managerial	103	63	85	1–3	37	46
Subtotal	319	181	181	1–3	103	126
N.R.	35	16	7	0	10	8
Total	354	197	188	1–3	113	134

TABLE 2.20.   Variation in Knowledge of Composers, by Father's Occupational Category (number of times composer's name is mentioned*)

Father's Occupation	Mozart	Beethoven	Bach	Brahms
Agriculture, industrial workers	62	66	60	54
Clerical, junior supervisory	127	129	122	105
Artisans, shopkeepers	91	88	86	74
Lower managerial	107	111	104	100
Senior managerial	240	232	221	205
Total	627	626	593	538

*Whether known through records or concerts.

TABLE 2.21.   The Political Spectrum: Philosophy

Age	Extreme Left Left %	Center %	Right Extreme Right %
under 21	68.5	22.5	9
21 to 25	69	15.5	15.5
over 25	44	50	6

4–10	8–10	Medians	Records					Median
			0	1–3	4–7	8–10	Total	
40	9	4–7	4	14	44	9	71	4–7
77	24	4–7	12	15	99	18	144	4–7
100	34	4–7	10	26	157	22	215	4–7
122	46	4–7	5	21	195	30	251	4–7
339	113	4–7	31	76	495	79	681	4–7
32	8	4–7	7	13	28	10	58	4–7
371	121	4–7	38	89	523	89	739	4–7

Debussy	Stravinsky	Chabrier	Palestrina	Weber	Boulez	Total number in category
38	29	21	7	8	1	71
91	78	57	20	13	1	142
62	56	31	21	9	2	97
85	80	38	14	19	3	118
191	167	83	42	33	9	245
467	410	230	104	82	16	673

TABLE 2.22. The Political Spectrum: Sociology

Age	Extreme Left Left %	Center %	Right Extreme Right %
under 21	51	29	20
21 to 25	60	24.5	15.5
over 25	76	22	2

TABLE 2.23. Religious Affiliation: Philosophy

Age	Catholic %	Non-Catholic %
under 21	68.5	31.5
21 to 25	81.5	18.5
over 25	91	9

TABLE 2.24. Religious Affiliation: Sociology

Age	Catholic %	Non-Catholic %
under 21	84	16
21 to 25	80	20
over 25	67.5	32.5

TABLE 2.25. Type of Accommodation

Age	Parents' Home %	Private Lodgings %	University Residence %	
under 21	57	30	13	(214)
21 to 25	30	58	12	(171)
over 25	10	78	12	(66)

TABLE 2.26. Part-time Job

Age	Job %	No Job %	
under 21	18	82	(214)
21 to 25	32.5	67.5	(171)
over 25	62	38	(66)

TABLE 2.27. Degree of Involvement: In Political Life

Age	Activist Member %	Sympathizer %	Indifferent %
under 21	15	58	27
21 to 25	27	49	24
over 25	21	69	10

TABLE 2.28. Degree of Involvement: In Student-Union Activity

Age	Official %	Member %	Indifferent Hostile %
under 21	12.5	57	30.5
21 to 25	16	53	31
over 25	27	62	11

TABLE 2.29. Type of Accommodation

Sex	Parents' Home %	Private Lodgings %	University Residence %	
M	34	52	14	(232)
F	46	43	11	(223)

TABLE 2.30. Part-time Job

Sex	Job %	No Job %
M	31	69
F	22	78

TABLE 2.31. Career Plans

Sex	Research %	Teaching %	Non-Academic Career %
M	20.9	61.5	17.6
F	13	80.5	6.5

TABLE 2.32. Students' Opinions of Their Own Academic Worth

Sex	Weak to Passable %	Fairly Good to Very Good %
M	36	64
F	53	47

TABLE 2.33. Nature of Books Read

Sex	Academic Texts %	Non-Academic Texts %
M	54	46
F	66	34

TABLE 2.34. Keeping a Catalog of Titles

Sex	Of Plays Seen %	Of Films Seen %	Of Concerts Heard %	Of Art Exhibitions %
M	10	17	5	3
F	19	27	9	8

TABLE 2.35. Involvement in Student Union

Sex	Official %	Member %	Indifferent Hostile %
M	23	54	23
F	7	58	35

TABLE 2.36. Involvement in Politics

Sex	Activist %	Member %	Indifferent Hostile %
M	29	51	20
F	12	60	28

TABLE 2.37. Female Student Political Involvement by Type of Accommodation

Type of Accommodation	Actively Involved %	Sympathizer %	Indifferent Hostile %
Parents' home	19.5	49.5	31
Private lodgings	32	38.5	29.5
University residence	46	25	29

TABLE 2.38. **Female Student Union Membership, by Type of Accommodation**

Type of Accommodation	Unionized %	Non Unionized %
Parents' home	53	47
Private lodgings	60	40
University residence	83	17

is very small at the level of ordinary membership, is greater at the level of involvement in responsibilities (tables 2.35 and 2.36).

Social Recruitment of Polish Universities (Table 2.39)

It can be seen that, from 1957, the proportion of students of working-class or peasant origin *accepted* into university ceases to be systematically higher than the proportion of *candidates* from these social categories. There is even the beginning of a tendency toward a decline in the share of workers' and peasants' children in university intake—from 30 percent to 27 percent for workers and from 24 percent to 19 percent for peasants. It can also be noted that, even in the case of a policy aimed at favoring lower-class enrollment, the peasant class remains disadvantaged relative to industrial workers: the proportion of new students whose fathers are workers is regularly greater than the proportion whose fathers are peasants, whereas, in the active population, workers in industry and construction account for 28 percent and agricultural workers 48 percent.[5]

Social Origin and Educational Opportunity in Hungary (Tables 2.40–2.43)

It can be seen that the chances of access to education are regularly greater for the children of senior executives and that this disparity is greater at higher levels of education. The children of senior executives are, in fact, two-and-a-half times more likely to enter the gymnasium and four times more likely to enter a university than the sons of manual workers. Type of secondary school also continues to be linked to social origin: when manual workers' children do receive secondary schooling, it is more likely to be in a technical school.

The influence of social origin (whether defined by father's occupational category or by the parents' highest educational qual-

TABLE 2.39. Social Origin of Candidates Accepted into First Year of University in Poland (1951–52 to 1961–62)[a]

Social Origin	1951–52 % Candidates	Accepted[b]	1952–53 % Candidates	Accepted	1953–54 % Candidates	Accepted	1954–55 % Candidates	Accepted	1955–56 % Candidates	Accepted	1956–57 % Candidates	Accepted
Workers	31.7	39.1	32.8	35.9	31.5	33.9	32.0	34.6	32.5	32.2	34.3	30.7
Peasants	22.2	24.9	23.8	25.1	24.9	25.9	24.4	24.4	25.0	24.0	25.1	22.0
Intelligentsia	46.1	36.0	43.4	39.0	43.6	40.2	43.6	41.0	42.5	43.8	40.6	47.3

	1957–58 % Candidates	Accepted	1958–59 % Candidates	Accepted	1959–60 % Candidates	Accepted	1960–61 % Candidates	Accepted	1961–62 % Candidates	Accepted
Workers	26.2	25.0	27.3	27.8	26.9	28.2	26.4	27.0	27.6	27.9
Peasants	21.6	21.1	21.0	21.3	20.1	20.1	19.0	19.3	18.9	19.4
Intelligentsia	52.2	53.9	51.7	50.9	53.0	51.7	54.6	53.7	53.5	52.7

[a]Based on Jan Szczepanski, *Socjologiczne Zagadnienia Wyższego Wykształcenia 1963.*
[b]The first figure indicates the number of candidates from the category as a percentage of the total number of candidates; the second figure indicates the number of students from the category who were accepted, as a percentage of the total number accepted.

TABLE 2.40. Proportion of Young People in Secondary and Higher Education in Hungary, by Father's Occupational Category*

Occupational Category of Head of Household	Per 1,000 Households			
	Pupils in Gymnasia	Pupils in Technical Schools	All Secondary Schools	University Students
Senior managerial, intellectuals	142	24	166	31
Other managerial	108	32	140	25
All managerial	121	29	150	28
Skilled workers	59	55	114	9
Semi-skilled	44	52	96	7
Unskilled	33	47	81	5
All manual workers	48	52	100	7
Total—all categories combined	69	46	115	13

*Based on a 1960 survey by Sandorne Ferge, *Statisztikai Szemle*, October 1962.

TABLE 2.41. School Marks and Social Origin in Hungary

Type of School	Average of Marks Awarded*		Managers' children's results compared to workers' children's results (%)
	Managers' Children	Workers' Children	
Grades 1 to 4 (primary school)	4.01	3.40	117.9
Primary school grades 5 to 8	3.72	3.16	117.7
Gymnasium	3.47	3.19	108.8

*The marks range from 1 to 5.

ification) can be seen from the first years of primary school to the gymnasium. The more favored a child's background, with respect to culture, the greater his chances of scholastic success. At later stages, the disparity in chances of success seems to decline (the superiority of the sons of managers falls from 117 percent in primary school to 108 percent in the gymnasium), but this, it must be remembered, is because the constant elimination of children from the disadvantaged strata brings together, in the gymnasium, managers' children and workers' children, who have been selected with unequal rigor.

TABLE 2.42. Hungary: Scholastic Performance and Father's Occupational Category*

Father's or Mother's Occupational Category	In Primary Schools				In Gymnasium French Lycée Grades 3–1	
	Grades 1–4		Grades 5–8			
	Best marks	Worst marks	Best marks	Worst marks	Best marks	Worst marks
Senior managerial, intellectuals	49	3	34	6	20	15
Other managerial	34	4	24	12	17	15
All managerial	40	4	28	10	18	14
Skilled workers	21	10	13	17	9	19
Semi-skilled	17	16	11	23	7	19
Unskilled	8	24	6	29	14	20
All manual workers	17	15	11	21	10	19

*Pupils in a social category who received best and worst marks, as percentage of total number of pupils in category.

TABLE 2.43. Hungary: Scholastic Performance and Parents' Educational Level*

Father's or Mother's Highest Qualification	In Primary Schools				In Gymnasia French Lycée Classes 3–1	
	Grades 1–4		Grades 5–8			
	Best marks	Worst marks	Best marks	Worst marks	Best marks	Worst marks
University degree	49	2	41	2	22	10
Baccalauréat	40	1	29	7	16	8
Eight grades (primary)	25	8	16	14	13	17
Less than eight grades	13	19	8	26	9	20

*Pupils in a social category who received best and worst marks, as percentages of total number of pupils in category.

Students and University Language (Tables 2.44–2.49)

To measure students' ability to understand and use the language of university teaching, we gave them a vocabulary test. The various exercises, devised on the basis of professorial discourse, such as it can be objectively observed, were aimed at exploring two dimensions of language use: on the one hand, *several areas* of vocabulary, from the most academic to those of everyday language or extracurricular culture; and, on the other hand, *several levels* of linguistic behavior, from the comprehension of a term in context to the most active forms of word manipulation, such as explicit awareness of multiple meanings or the ability to formulate a complete definition.

This survey revealed two basic facts: the extent of linguistic misunderstanding in higher education and the crucial role of linguistic inheritance. But it is impossible to give a complete, systematic explanation of all the differences brought to light by analytical criteria such as social origin, sex, or various characteristics of students' educational history, unless allowance is made for the fact that the populations divided by these criteria have been *unequally selected* in the course of their previous schooling. Thus, the relationships uncovered by statistical analysis are not—contrary to appearances—established between a group defined by the criteria which constitute it, and a level of success. For example, scores in a language test are never the mark of students characterized solely by their previous training, their social origin, and their sex, or even by the combination of all these criteria, but, rather, of the group which, precisely because it has these characteristics, has not been eliminated by failure to the same extent as a group defined by other characteristics. In other words, it is a fallacy to suppose that one can directly and exclusively identify even the cross-influence of factors such as social origin or sex, in synchronic relations which, in the case of a population defined by a certain past, take on their full significance only in the context of the educational *trajectory*.

If the disadvantage attached to social origin is mainly mediated through the type of secondary school course to which a child is assigned, it is not surprising that the children of senior executives should have the best scores when they have had either the most classical or least classical secondary training, whereas the working-class students come off best in the subgroup of "Latinists." The fact that the latter have studied Latin is probably due to some untypical feature of their family background, and, given that they belong to a category in which this subject option is more rare, they have had to manifest exceptional qualities to have been channeled in this direction and to have stayed there. An analogous phenomenon is seen in the subgroup defined by the most classical schooling, where the working-class students have results virtually equal to those of *all* students who have done Latin and Greek

TABLE 2.44. Linguistic Competence, by Social Origin and Type of Secondary Schooling

	Neither Greek nor Latin				Latin			Latin and Greek			Combined		
	Working class	Lower middle class	Upper class		Working class	Lower middle class	Upper class	Working class	Lower middle class	Upper class	Working class	Lower middle class	Upper class
Score less than 12/20	52	54	39		48	58	52	38.5	55	26.5	46	55	57.5
Score 12/20 and over	48	46	61		52	42	48	61.5	45	73.5	54	45	42.5

(61.5 percent, as against 62 percent overall), and slightly lower than those of the upper-class students (73.5 percent). This is explained by the fact that in this subgroup, they are competing with the group of well-heeled students who have exercised their privilege and made the most of their school option, thanks to the countless advantages bestowed by a cultured background.

TABLES 2.45 and 2.46.   Linguistic Competence by Social Origin and Residence in Paris or Provinces

	Paris			Provinces			Combined		
	Working class %	Lower Middle class %	Upper class %	Working class %	Lower Middle class %	Upper class %	Working class %	Lower Middle class %	Upper class %
Score less than 12/20	9	31	35	54	60	41	46	55	42.5
Score 12/20 and over	91	69	65	46	40	59	54	45	57.5

		Linguistic advantages	Selection implied in university entrance		Linguistic level
Working class	Paris	—	+ +	→	+
	Provinces	— —	+	→	—
Lower middle class	Paris	—	+	→	0 (+)
	Provinces	— —	0	→	— —
Upper class	Paris	+ +	— —	→	0
	Provinces	+	—	→	0

The + and — signs define the relative values which situate the three groups in terms of the phenomenon considered in each column, with 0 defining the intermediate position.

If the logic is followed through, it is to be expected that the relationship between the hierarchy of language test results and the hierarchy of social backgrounds would tend to be progressively reversed as the selection of the disadvantaged classes becomes more severe. And as a matter of fact, while Parisian students, from whatever background, score higher than provincial students, the difference is most marked among working-class students (Paris, 91 percent; provinces, 46 percent; as against 65 percent and 59 percent for the upper classes). In Paris, the working-class students have the best results, followed by the lower-middle-class and upper-class students. To understand this reversal of the usual relationship, it has to be borne in mind that the cultural atmosphere associated with living in Paris is combined with linguistic advantages and also with a more severe selection. If the linguistic advantages deriving from family background and the severity of selection in the different cases are defined in terms of relative values (+ or −), then one only has to add up these values in order to account for the hierarchy of language test results (see table 2.46).

TABLE 2.47. **Linguistic Competence by Sex and Type of Secondary Schooling**

	Neither Greek nor Latin		Latin		Latin and Greek		Combined	
	M %	F %	M %	F %	M %	F %	M %	F %
Score less than 12/20	34	60	39	58.5	41.5	96	38	54
12/20 and over	66	40	61	41.5	58.5	64	62	46

Since the percentages are calculated within each column, we have emphasized the stronger tendency on each line within each type of secondary schooling.

Even the apparent exception can be understood in terms of the relationship between degree of selection and degree of success. Whereas male students who have studied neither Latin nor Greek, or only Latin, score better than similarly trained female students, the girls do better within the "Hellenist" group (64 percent of them, as against 50.5 percent of the men, score more than the median mark). This inversion of the usual difference is undoubtedly explained by the fact that girls are less likely than boys to receive this training, so that those who do receive it are more highly selected than similarly trained men.

If the linguistic advantages which stem from social origin and the rate of selection which university entrance and, secondarily, entry to the Arts faculty imply for students of each sex and each social class are again defined in relative values, it can be seen that one only has to combine these values to account for the hierarchy of the various groups' results in the definition test.

TABLES 2.48 and 2.49. Linguistic Competence by Sex and Social Origin

		Linguistic advantages	Selection implied by university entrance	Selection implied by entering Arts faculty		Linguistic level
Working class	M	—	+	+	→	+
	F	—	+ +	— —	→	—
Lower middle class	M	—	0	+	→	0
	F	—	0	—	→	— —
Upper class	M	+ +	— —	+ +	→	+ +
	F	+ +	— —	—	→	—

	Working class		Lower middle class		Upper class		Combined	
	M %	F %	M %	F %	M %	F %	M %	F %
Less than 12/20	35.5	53.5	43	60.5	33	47	38	54
12/20 and over	64.5	46.5	57	39.5	67	53	62	46

The expression of the relative degrees of selection in terms of + and — is an approximate rendering of the data obtained by calculating the various subgroups' chances of entering university and conditional chances of entering the Arts faculty (see p. 3).

The Differential Yield from an Academic Heritage (Table 2.50)

To measure the differential advantage derived from belonging to a teaching family, we have compared the number of students in each faculty who are the children of university or lycée teachers with the total number of students in that faculty who are the children of senior executives (ratio I), and compared the number of students who are the children of primary school teachers (or the equivalent) with the total number of students who are the children of lower-rank executives (ratio II). When these ratios are compared with the ratio of university and secondary teachers to all senior executives and the ratio of primary teachers to lower-rank executives in the working population (1/7 and 1/5, respectively), it can be seen that teachers' children are not more than proportionately represented (at both levels of stratification), except in the Arts and Science faculties.

TABLE 2.50.   Teachers' Children in the Various Faculties

	Arts	Science	Medicine	Pharmacy	Law	Combined	Working population
Ratio I	$\dfrac{1}{3.2}$	$\dfrac{1}{7.4}$	$\dfrac{1}{8.6}$	$\dfrac{1}{11.7}$	$\dfrac{1}{12.8}$	$\dfrac{1}{6}$	$\dfrac{1}{7.4}$
Ratio II	$\dfrac{1}{2.8}$	$\dfrac{1}{3.2}$	$\dfrac{1}{3.2}$	$\dfrac{1}{3.7}$	$\dfrac{1}{3.7}$	$\dfrac{1}{9.1}$	$\dfrac{1}{5.3}$

Relegation to Science Faculties (Tables 2.51–2.53)

Industrial workers' children are more strongly represented in the Science faculties than in Arts faculties. Moreover, it was the Science faculties that benefited more than all others from the relative democratization of recruitment between 1960 and 1965. The proportion of industrial workers' children rose from 8.5 percent to 15 percent in these faculties, whereas, over the same period, it increased from 7 percent to 11 percent in higher education as a whole. But it is impossible to explain this phenomenon completely without considering the other educational possibilities open to Science students, particularly the preparatory classes for the *grandes écoles*. While industrial workers' sons, whose chances of entering higher education are very slender, are most likely to study science if they are admitted, it has to be noted that only very exceptionally do they head for the *classes préparatoires*, where they make up only 6 percent of the student body. And in the *grandes écoles* themselves, they are even less strongly represented: 1.9 percent at the Ecole Normale Supérieure (ENS) and 2 percent at the Ecole Polytechnique. Thus, the apparently more democratic intake of the Science faculties, in fact, masks a relegation.

Furthermore, the mechanism which channels working-class students into Science faculties is already at work when they enter secondary school. They are most often consigned to Collèges d'Enseignement Générale (CEG), in other words, to the "modern" section, and, therefore, can at best endeavor to experience their forced choice as a vocation.

The same process of relegation is found even within the Science faculties. The hierarchy of the prestige of the different sections, as established by academic consensus, more or less coincides with the hierarchy of their students' social origins. Thus, working-class students are more strongly represented as one moves down the prestige hierarchy of the sections. These few examples suffice to

TABLE 2.51. Social Origin of Science Students in the Various Higher-Education Establishments

	Science faculties (1964–65) %	Classes pré-paratoires (1963–64) %	E N S Science (1965–66) %
Farmers	8.5	3.4	2.9
Industrial workers	13.5	6.0	1.9
Clerical workers	9.5	6.2	2.9
Artisans and shopkeepers	13.5	7.2	8.9
Lower-rank executives	22.0	16.0	16.0
Senior executives	33.0	61.2	67.4
Total	100	100	100

TABLE 2.52. Type of School at Start of Secondary Schooling and Section Entered

	CEG %	Private School %	Lycée %	Modern %	Classical %
Farmers	51.5	20.0	28.5	73.0	27.0
Industrial workers	59.0	5.5	35.5	80.0	20.0
Clerical workers	46.0	11.5	42.5	68.5	31.5
Artisans and shopkeepers	40.0	17.5	42.5	68.0	32.0
Lower-rank executives	35.0	10.5	54.5	63.0	37.0
Primary teachers	33.5	3.5	63.0	49.0	51.0
Senior executives	14.0	24.0	62.0	31.5	68.5
Scientific administrators	15.5	28.5	56.0	36.5	63.5
Professors	7.5	12.0	80.5	16.5	83.5

TABLE 2.53. Section in Science Faculty, by Social Origin

	Natural Sciences, Physics, and Chemistry	Mathematics, Physics, and Chemistry	General, Mathematics, and Physics
Farmers	31	45	24
Industrial workers	23	49	28
Clerical workers	24	49	27
Artisans and shopkeepers	24	47	29
Lower-rank executives	25	41	34
Primary teachers	23	40	37
Senior executives	24	39	37
Scientific executives	21	31	48
Professors	21	23	56

show that the mechanisms ensuring the transmission of cultural inheritance are not essentially different from those which have been described for the Arts faculties, although they take a specific form.[6]

Notes

Prefatory Note

1. Pierre Bourdieu and Jean-Claude Passeron, *Les étudiants et leurs études*, Cahiers du centre de sociologie européenne (Paris, The Hague: Mouton, 1964).

2. Institut national de la statistique et des études économiques: Bureau universitaire de statistique.

3. See below, p 8.

Chapter 1

1. See table 1 and figs. 1 and 2. The appendixes to this volume contain various statistics on the student population and a note on the method used to calculate the chances of entering higher education and the likelihood of taking a particular course, by social origin and sex.

2. These comments are intended to indicate the trends observable in the conditional probabilities, which almost always order students' chances as a function of their social origin. However, it must be noted that the clerical worker category often contradicts the most pronounced trends. For example, the likelihood of studying Medicine is greater for the sons and daughters of clerical workers than for the sons and daughters of lower-rank executives; and the sons and daughters of office workers also have the greatest conditional likelihood of studying Law. We undoubtedly see here some of the consequences of the attitude of the lower stratum of the petite bourgeoisie toward education and social ascent.

3. See table 2.

4. See appendix 2, table 2.11.

5. See appendix 2, tables 2.51–2.53.

6. See p. 26.

7. "Talas" (student slang: "ceux qui von*t à la* messe") and "non talas" or "anti-talas" (trans. note).

8. See appendix 2, tables 2.21–2.28.

9. See appendix 2, tables 2.1–2.5.

10. The work of Basil Bernstein has shown how the structure of the language spoken in working-class families acts as a cultural obstacle (see for example "Social Structure, Language and Learning," *Educational Research* 3 (June 1961): 163–76. A vocabulary test designed to grasp the factors which underlie the performance of philosophy and sociology students in various types of language handling—the ability to define words, explicit awareness of multiple meanings, the ability to give synonyms—shows that the most classical secondary training (Latin and Greek) is the basic variable most strongly tied to linguistic mastery. The more scholastic the exercise, the greater the correlation, which is highest of all in the definition exercise (see the first part of *Rapport pédagogique et communication*, Cahiers du CSE, no. 2 The Hague, Paris: Mouton, 1965). Thus, the disadvantage attached to social origin is mainly transmitted through the choice of courses, with success at the highest level of the educational system remaining closely tied to the most remote scholastic past. Detailed examination of the test results also shows that the performance of students from the various social classes can only be understood in terms of the logic of the continuous conversion of social heritage into academic heritage in different class situations. For example, the test results of senior executives' children tend to be distributed bimodally, thereby revealing that this statistical category in fact conceals two groups differentiated by their cultural orientations and, no doubt, by secondary social characteristics. Again, working-class students come out top in the subcategory of Latinists, and this is because the rarity of such a training implies a relative overselection of these students (see appendix 2, table 2.44).

11. See fig. 3 and appendix 2, tables 2.6–2.13.

12. When students of bourgeois origin are invited to express their opinions about their own academic worth by rating themselves on a scale, they are less likely than lower-class students to place themselves in the "average" category (75 percent as against 88 percent) and more readily describe themselves as "good" or "very good" (18 percent as against 10 percent), while petit-bourgeois students have intermediate attitudes in all these cases. In this same group, the working-class students have academic records which are usually better than those of the upper-class students: 58 percent of them have had at least one distinction in past examinations, compared to 39 percent for the upper-class students, and the gap is even more manifest in the group of students with at least two distinctions, since there are proportionately twice as many working-class students there, 33.5 percent compared to 18 percent.

13. See fig. 4 and appendix 2, tables 2.14–2.20.

14. High social origin does not automatically and equally favor all those who have the benefit of it. In the case of theater and concert

attendance, the children of senior executives are distributed bimodally. The scores of part of this group (approximately a third of them) set it apart from the rest of the category as well as from the rest of the student population. See appendix 2, tables 2.14 and 2.19.

15. Empirical inquiry can only ever grasp these significant totalities in the form of successive profiles, since it has to rely on indicators which fragment the object of analysis.

16. The contradiction involved in the laborious winning of a "gift" can be seen in the psychological and intellectual dramas to which this miracle condemns its victims. Péguy, for example, can be seen as a man whose only way of overcoming the uneasy awareness of his election was to transfigure it in his literary oeuvre, the mythical solution to his social drama.

17. Ms. S. Ferge, of the Hungarian Central Statistics Office, suggested to us the use of this indicator of educational opportunity at the level of the family, that is, in a form in which the subject can perceive it concretely. The extended family included the grandparents, parents, sibs, parents' sibs, and first cousins. The difference found between the chances of higher education typical of a social stratum and the real number of members of the extended families of students belonging to that category who are or have been in higher education is the more significant in that the enrollment rate has risen steadily from one generation to another.

Chapter 2

1. See appendix 1, tables 1.3 and 1.4.

2. See appendix 2, tables 2.12 and 2.13.

3. *Corporative*: a kind of student mutual benefit society (trans.).

4. A student population always gives a particularly high rate of nonresponses to the question about parents' occupations.

5. In reply to an open-ended question, three-quarters of the students associated the most important event in their aesthetic biography with a teacher.

6. An annual competition for *lycéens* (trans.).

7. A student at the *Ecole Normale Supérieure* (trans.).

8. The mystique of academic success as a sign of personal salvation reaches its peak in the classes preparing for the *grandes écoles*, especially in Arts disciplines. The dramas provoked by certain failures— and, equally, certain successes—are well known.

9. Mme. Amado Lévy-Valensi, "L'étudiant possède-t-il une affectivité d'adulte?" *Lille-U*, no. 7 (Nov.-Dec. 1963).

10. This is a simplified model of the relations within the student-union bureaucracy, e.g. the relationship of a branch in the Paris group to the FGEL (*Fédération des groupes d'études de lettres*) and of the

FGEL to the UNEF leadership (*Union nationale des étudiants de France*).

11. We touch on this debate here only because sociological analysis finds in the oppositions between scientific and literary organizations, or between Parisian and provincial ones, something other and more than clashes between theses that are amenable solely to political judgment. These conflicts can be seen to express, if not really opposed interests, then at least differences in spirit closely linked to social differences between the conflicting groups.

12. See fig. 5.

Chapter 3

1. It may be objected that we define here only one of the possible rationalities of education, and especially of higher education. The rational type of relation to study of which we outline some features here is nothing other than the ideal type of intellectual apprenticeship, to which it is possible to refuse to reduce studenthood, for the most plausible of reasons. But this minimum definition is featured here because, in the charismatic representation of study which students and teachers tend to construct, it is the one that is most completely refused. It will be seen below that traditional or charismatic vestiges can have a positive function, especially in the most traditional disciplines, such as literature or philosophy (see pp. 58–59).

2. The definition of "rational" education implicitly offered here through an *ideal-typical* description of rational apprenticeship might be contested on the grounds that the demands of the economic system are no longer formulated in terms of narrow specialization and that the emphasis is on adaptability to various tasks. But this is only a verbal quibble, since what is involved is, at bottom, a type of specialization demanded by changes in the economic system. However, our intention is not to advocate a strictly specialized education, which would amount to sanctioning cultural inequalities, since the family would then be the only vehicle of high culture. The ambiguities of schooling are the more sinister in that no institution can take the place of the school when it comes to introducing the greatest number to culture in all its forms, from museum-going to the handling of economic notions and techniques or political consciousness. The fact that arts and letters are generally taught by traditional methods (precisely on account of the social function of that culture) should not lead one to the conclusion that there could not be here, as elsewhere, a rational pedagogy.

3. These virtues have their excesses, which are derided by teachers and students alike: obsessive "swotting" (*polarisation*) and charlatanism (*fumisterie*).

4. For a more systematic analysis of the pedagogic relationship as a complicitous exchange of prestigious images and of the accompanying tolerance of linguistic misunderstanding, see the introduction to *Rapport pédagogique et communication*, pp. 11–36.

5. See appendix 1, table 1.5.

6. The way the number of female students in the different disciplines has changed over the years shows that the traditional models of the division of labor between the sexes still very strongly govern female students' career choices and thereby dominate their experience of their situation. The proportion of female students is greatest (more than one in two), and the feminization has been most rapid, in the Arts faculties (where women gained a foothold very early) and in Pharmacy. See appendix 1, table 1.5.

7. See appendix 2, tables 2.31–2.34.

8. See appendix 2, tables 2.35 and 2.36.

Conclusion

1. When we emphasize the *ideological function* which recourse to the idea of unequal giftedness fulfills in certain conditions, we do not mean to contest the natural inequality of human abilities, although we see no reason why the random processes of genetics should not distribute these unequal gifts equally among the different social classes. But this is an abstract self-evidence, and sociological research has a duty to suspect and methodically expose the socially conditioned cultural inequality beneath apparent natural inequalities, since it can only fall back on "nature" when all other explanation fails. So there are never grounds for being certain of the natural character of the inequalities found between persons in a given social situation and, as regards education, until all the ways in which the social factors of inequality operate have been explored and all the pedagogic means of counteracting them have been exhausted, it is better to doubt too much than too little.

2. It is no accident that challenging the natural gift ideology leads one into the logic by which the Kantian ethic of merit opposed the classical morality of innate virtues, the exclusive endowment of the well-born.

3. See appendix 2, table 2.39.

Epilogue

For an account and selective bibliography of research since 1964 by the Centre for European Sociology, see P. Bourdieu and J.-C. Passeron, *Reproduction in Education, Culture and Society* (London and Beverly

Hills: Sage, 1977), pp. xv–xviii and 237–41. For the full, original
text of this study, with all the supporting data, see P. Bourdieu "Classe-
ment, déclassement, reclassement," *Actes de la Recherche en Sciences
Sociales* no. 24 (November 1978): 2–22.

1. To the effects of the competition between groups struggling for
"upclassing" and against "downclassing," a competition that is organized around the academic qualification [*titre*], and in a more general
way around all the "entitlements" by which groups assert and constitute their own scarcity-value vis-à-vis other groups, must be added
the effect of what might be called a *structural* factor. Generally increased schooling has the effect of increasing the mass of cultural
capital, which, at every moment, exists in an "embodied" state. We
know that the success of the school's educative action and the dur-
ability of its effects depend on how much cultural capital has been
directly transmitted by the family, so we can presume that the efficiency
of school-based educative action tends to rise constantly, other things
being equal. In short, the same scholastic investment becomes more
profitable, a fact which no doubt contributes to inflation by bringing
diplomas within reach of a greater number of people.

2. Habitus: a system of durably acquired schemes of perception,
thought, and action, engendered by objective conditions but tending to
persist even after an alteration of those conditions (hysteresis). See P.
Bourdieu, *Outline of a Theory of Practice* (Cambridge: Cambridge
University Press, 1977). (Translator's note.)

3. *Allodoxia:* an alternative system of taken-for-granted assump-
tions, running counter to the implicit consensus (*doxa*). (Translator's
note.)

4. *Certificat d'études:* primary schooling certificate; BEPC: *Brevet
d'études du premier cycle du second degré,* certifying completion of the
first part of secondary schooling.

5. To make clear the break with the realist, fixist model implied in
certain traditions of the sociology of work, it has to be emphasized that
the *post* cannot be reduced either to the theoretical post, i.e., as described in regulations, circulars, or organization charts, or to the real
post, i.e., as described on the basis of observation of the occupant's
real function, or even to the relationship between the two. In fact, posts,
as regards both their theoretical definition and their practical reality,
are the site of permanent struggles, in which position-holders may
clash with their superiors or their subordinates, or with the occupants
of neighboring and rival positions, or amongst themselves (e.g., old-
timers and newcomers, graduates and nongraduates, and so on). Those
aspiring to or holding a position may have an interest in redefining it
in such a way that it cannot be occupied by anyone other than the
possessors of properties identical to their own.

6. *Hexis:* mode of physical being, bearing, as opposed to *praxis.* (Translator's note.)

7. *Sixième:* first grade of secondary schooling. (Translator's note.)

8. *Allodoxia:* see above, note 3.

9. L. Stone, "The Inflation of Honours, 1558–1641," *Past and Present* 14 (1958): 45–70.

10. The limiting case of such processes of statistical action is represented by processes of panic or *rout,* in which each agent helps to produce what he fears by performing actions inspired by the feared effect (as happens in financial panics). In all such cases, the collective action, the mere statistical sum of uncoordinated individual actions, leads to a collective result irreducible or contrary to the collective interest and even to the particular interests pursued by the individual actions.

11. Cf. L. Stone, "Theories of Revolution," *World Politics* 18, no. 2 (January 1966): 159–76.

Appendix 1

1. This documentation was compiled at the Centre for European Sociology, Paris, from data supplied by the Institut national de la statistique et des études économiques (INSEE) and the Bureau universitaire de statistique (BUS).

2. Raymond Aron, "Sur quelques problèmes des universités françaises," *Archives européennes de sociologie* 3 (1962): 102–22.

3. The 1914–18 war produced a surge in the rate of female attendance in the faculties, which varied in strength among the disciplines and fell back after the war, except in Pharmacy.

4. If we take as an indicative threshold the moment when the proportion of female students definitively passes the 20 percent mark (that is, setting aside the temporary increase in female students during wartime), we find that the line is crossed in the following order: Arts, Pharmacy, Science, Medicine, Law. This is roughly the same order as is obtained by considering the rate of growth in the proportion of female students in the various disciplines: Arts and Pharmacy, then Science, then Law and Medicine.

5. These are rough estimates obtained by comparing the 19–24-year-old student population with the total numbers in the corresponding age groups. For the years 1911, 1936, and 1946, there are no statistics providing a breakdown of the student population by age. On the basis that the 19–24 age band represents, on average, for the period 1950–62, 65 percent of the student population, we have assumed that it represented the same proportion in the previous years and also in 1960 and 1963 (years for which there is again no breakdown by age). Also, the rate of enrollment thus obtained is very slightly underestimated, since it fails to include the students enrolled in some of the

grandes écoles and in various institutes attached to the faculties or universities and also the secondary-school pupils in the same category (for example, the *classes préparatoires*—trans.).

6. The 19–24 age group in the French population declined slightly, from 3,707,000 in 1911, to 3,420,700 in 1963.

7. Students aged 17 or below accounted for less than 3 percent of the numbers in higher education.

8. By Alain Darbel, Director of the INSEE.

9. *Cohort* is meant in the demographic sense.

Appendix 2

1. The survey findings used in this appendix are selected from the full results published in P. Bourdieu and J.-C. Passeron, *Les étudiants et leurs études* (Paris, The Hague: Mouton, 1964).

2. The indicators of the influence of social origin used below may appear debatable or unusual, precisely because a limited set has been chosen and because their evidential force lies in the fact that they indicate a system of variations which are always distributed in the same way.

3. Some of these combinations are classic (Law plus Sociology), others more unexpected: Modern Languages (or Literature) plus Sociology. It is not uncommon for students from the most well-to-do strata to combine courses from more than two disciplines and several faculties or institutes.

4. A compulsory preparatory course between the *baccalauréat* and entry to some faculties and *grandes écoles*, 1948–66 (trans.).

5. *Rocznik Statystyczny* 1962: Breakdown of active population in Poland in 1960.

6. See M. de Saint-Martin, "Les facteurs de l'élimination et de la sélection différentielles dans les études de sciences", *Revue française de sociologie*, 9, special no., (1968): 167–84.